# SCOTTISH

# SOLDIERS

# IN

# COLONIAL

# AMERICA

### Part One
### and
### Part Two

by David Dobson

GW00676305

## CLEARFIELD

David Dobson
8 Lawhead Road West
St Andrews
Fife, Scotland KY16 9NE

# SCOTTISH SOLDIERS IN COLONIAL AMERICA

## Part One

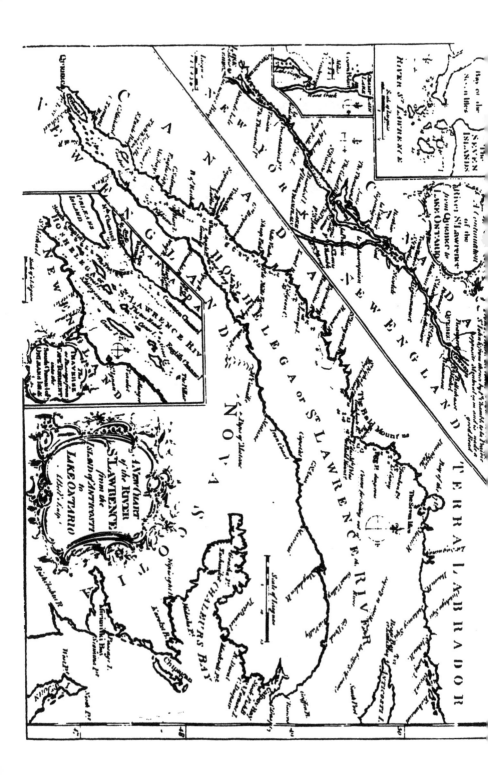

# INTRODUCTION

From as early as the 1650s there were Scots serving in the colonial militia forces of New England and possibly of Virginia. These men had arrived in America in chains as prisoners of war captured after Worcester and other battles of the Civil War and subsequently transported to the colonies as indentured servants. However it was not until the mid eighteenth century that the British Government began to despatch Highland Regiments, such as Fraser's Highlanders, the Black Watch, and Montgomery's Highlanders to America. The Seven Years War 1756-1763, otherwise known as the French and Indian War, led to significant recruitment in Scotland, particularly in the Highlands, for service in the American colonies. The experience gained by these soldiers was to influence their decision to subsequently settle or emigrate to America. The allocation of land to former military personnel in the aftermath of the war was a major incentive. The massive increase in emigration to America from the Highlands that occurred in the decade after the Seven Years War resulted to some extent from the influence of returning soldiers. On the outbreak of the American War of Independence, alias the American Revolution, former soldiers who had received land grants were recalled for duty by the British Government. For example many former Scottish soldiers who had been settled in the Mohawk Valley in upper New York were recruited into the King's Royal Regiment of New York. At the same time many new or recent immigrants from Scotland formed the Royal Highland Emigrant Regiment. After the war large numbers of soldiers from Loyalist units and from regular British Army regiments, including many Scots, were settled in what have become Nova Scotia, Prince Edward Island, New Brunswick, Ontario and Quebec. Scottish soldiers thus not only played an important role in defending the American colonies but also a prominent role in settling them. This book, the first of a series, attempts to identify individual soldiers and is based on research into both manuscript and printed material.

David Dobson
St Andrews, 1995

# REFERENCES

## ARCHIVES

| | | |
|---|---|---|
| MCA | Montgomery County Archives, New York | |
| | DFpp Duncan Fraser Papers | |
| PRO | Public Record Office, London | |
| | AO | Audit Office |
| | CO | Colonial Office |
| | PCC | Prerogative Court of Canterbury |
| SRO | Scottish Record Office, Edinburgh | |
| | CS | Court of Session |
| | GD | Gifts and Deposits |
| NRAS | National Register of Archives, Scotland | |
| | RH | Register House |
| | RS | Register of Sasines |

## PUBLICATIONS

| | |
|---|---|
| BM | Blackwood's Magazine, series, Edinburgh |
| BOM | Book of Mackay, A.Mackay, [Edinburgh, 1936] |
| CA | Chronicles of Atholl and Tullibardine, John, Duke of Atholl, [Edinburgh, 1908] |
| DPCA | Dundee, Perth and Cupar Advertiser, series |
| F | Fasti Ecclesiae Scoticanae, J. Scott. [Edinburgh, 1915-] |
| NY.Col.MS. | Manuscripts Illustrative of the Colonial History of New York J O'Callaghan, [New York, 1852] |
| OBW | Officers of the Black Watch, 1725-1952, [Perth, 1952] |
| PCCol | Calendar of the Privy Council, Colonial |
| RSF | History of the Royal Scots Fusiliers, 1678-1918, J. Buchan, [London, 1923] |
| SHS | Sketches of the Highlanders of Scotland, Major General David Stewart, [Edinburgh, 1825] |
| SM | Scots Magazine, series, [Edinburgh] |
| TGSI | Transactions of the Gaelic Society of Inverness, series |

# SCOTTISH SOLDIERS
# IN COLONIAL AMERICA

ABERCROMBY, JAMES, of Glassa, Captain of the 42nd Highlanders
16.2.1756, at New York 22.5.1757, ADC to Major General
Amherst 5.1759, Major of the 78th {Fraser Highlanders} Regiment
7.1760, retired 1763, Lieutenant Colonel of the 22nd Regiment in
America 3.1770, killed at Bunker's Hill 17.6.1775
[NYSHA.X][OBW16]

ALSTON, ......, Lieutenant of the 80th Regiment, died at Jamestown,
Virginia, 1781 [Edinburgh Evening Courant, 3.10 1781]
[SRO.GD1.394/30]

ANDERSON, WILLIAM, private in the 42nd Highlanders [Captain Reid's
Company} in New York 10.1757. [CA.3.440]

ARNOT, HUGH, Lieutenant of the 42nd Highlanders 4.1756, in New
York 22.5 1757, at Ticonderoga 1758. [NYSHA.X]

BAILLIE, ALEXANDER, Captain of the 21st {Royal Scots Fusiliers}
Regiment, to America 1776, surrendered at Saratoga 17 10 1777
[RSF]

BAILLIE, WILLIAM, Lieutenant of the Royal Regiment of Highlanders,
in New York 22.5.1757, killed at Ticonderoga 7 1758.
Pro. 7.1759 PCC [NYSHA.X][OBW17][SM.XX.437]

BAILLIE, ....., Captain of Fraser's Highlanders, killed at Louisbourg
6.1758. [SM.XX.435]

BAIN, ROBERT, sawyer, 42nd Highlanders, at Crown Point 16.8.1759
[NYSHA.X]

BALFOUR, HENRY, Captain of the 1st {Royal Scots} Regiment,
allocated 5,000 acres of land in New York 2.1765 [PC Col.V.818]

BALFOUR, JAMES, army officer in St Vincent and in New York 1775-
1776. [SRO.NRAS.0227.28-30]

BALNEAVIS, PATRICK, son of Balneavis of Edradour, Ensign of the
42nd Highlanders 1.1756, in New York 22.5 1757, wounded at
Ticonderoga 7.1758, and at Martinique 1762, Captain-Lieutenant
1763-1770. [NYSHA.X][OBW18][SM.XX.437]

BARCLAY, SIMON, Lieutenant of the 42nd Highlanders, embarked for
America 11.1757, killed in Martinique. [NYSHA.X]

BARRON, JAMES, soldier of the 84th {Royal Highland Emigrant}
Regiment in New York 15.7 1778. [SRO.GD174.2120.3/4]

BLACKWOOD, JOHN, Lieutenant of the 21st {Royal Scots Fusiliers} Regiment, to America 1776, surrendered at Saratoga 17.10.1777. [RSF]

BLAIR, SIMON, Lieutenant of the 42nd Highlanders embarked for New York 11.1757, died in Havanna 1762. [NYSHA.X][OBW20]

BOWDEN, JAMES, born in Scotland 1752, soldier of the 2nd Battalion Royal Highlanders in Philadelphia 20.5.1778.[SRO.GD174.2120.2]

BREMNER, GEORGE. late of the 42nd Regiment, granted 200 acres east of the River Hudson, Albany County, New York, 13.2.1767. [NY Col. MS.7.905]

BRODIE, GEORGE, Captain of the 21st {Royal Scots Fusiliers} Regiment, to America 1776, surrendered at Saratoga 17.10.1777. [RSF]

BRUCE, JAMES, soldier, 42nd Highlanders, at Crown Point, 27.8.1759 [NYSHA.X]

BRYDEN, ROBERT, born in Scotland 1750, soldier of the 2nd Battalion Royal Highlanders in New York 15.7.1778. [SRO.GD174.2120.2]

BUCHANAN, JOHN, private in the 42nd Highlanders {Captain Reid's Company} in New York 10.1757, killed in action. [CA.3.440]

BURD, JAMES, late Colonel of a Provincial Regiment in Pennsylvania, 19 6 1760. [SRO.RS27.173 177]

BURNETT, Sir ROBERT, of Leys, born 20.12.1755, Lieutenant of the 21st {Royal Scots} Fusiliers in America 1776, surrendered at Saratoga 17.10.1777-, died 1 1837. ["Family of Burnett of Leys" Aberdeen, 1891}][RSF]

CAMERON, ALEXANDER, born in Glenmoriston 1727, emigrated from Fort William to America on the Pearl 1773, settled on the Kingsborough Patent, New York, Loyalist, soldier of the Royal Regiment of New York 1780-1783, settled in Cornwall, Ontario, died 1.1823 [DFpp]

CAMERON, ALLAN, Corporal of the 2nd Foot, died in New Jersey [Pro. 6.1765 PCC]

CAMERON, ANGUS, private in the 42nd Highlanders {Captain Reid's Company} in New York 10 1757. [CA.3 440]

CAMERON, CHARLES, Captain of the 71st Regiment, died in Savannah, Georgia, 1779 son of Charles Cameron in Kilmally, Scotland. [Pro. 1.1782 PCC][SHS.2.112]

CAMERON, HUGH, private in the 42nd Highlanders {Captain Reid's Company} in New York 10.1757, killed in action. [CA.3.440]

CAMERON, HUGH, emigrated to America 1774, settled on the Kingsborough Patent, New York, Loyalist, soldier of the Royal Regiment of New York, settled in Cornwall, Ontario. [DFpp]

CAMERON, JOHN, born 1732, a deserter from Captain John de Garmo's
Company in New York 1764. [New York Mercury, 12.3.1764]

CAMERON, RONALD, soldier of the 2nd Battalion Royal Highlanders in
Philadelphia 20.5 1778, in New York 15.7.1778.
[SRO.GD174.2120.2/3]

CAMERON, ...., Ensign of the 71st Regiment, killed in South Carolina
1780. [SM.XXXXII.265]

CAMPBELL, ALEXANDER, son of Patrick Campbell of Barcaldine and
Lucia Cameron, a Lieutenant and possibly a Captain in Loudoun's
Highlanders in 1757, wounded at Louisbourg 1758, died in Quebec
1759. [TGSI.XXI.126][SM.XX.435]

CAMPBELL, Major ALEXANDER, born 1729, son of John Campbell of
Barcaldine, at Fort Duquesne 1759 [SRO GD87 1/84]; Major of
Montgomery's Highlanders 1757, Lieutenant Colonel of the 48th
Regiment 1759, [TGSI.XXI.127]; Lieutenant Colonel of Colonel
Burton's Regiment in South Carolina 1761. [SRO GD87.1/89]; died
in Bath 22.4.1779.

CAMPBELL, Major ALEXANDER, son of Duncan Campbell of Glenure,
from Greenock to New York 6.1774, wounded at Bunker's Hill
6.1775, at Hampton Road, Virginia, 20.2.1776
[SRO GD170.1595/13; 1063/24-25]

CAMPBELL, ALEXANDER, son of Campbell of Inverawe, Lieutenant of
the 42nd Highlanders in New York 22.5.1757, wounded at
Ticonderoga 7.1758. [NYSHA.X][SM.XX.437]

CAMPBELL, ALAN, drummer of the 42nd Highlanders {Captain John
Reid's Company} in New York 10.1757. [CA.3 440]

CAMPBELL, ALLAN, to New York on the Lyon 6.1757, at Ticonderoga
and Crown Point 1759. [SRO.GD170.1465; 1067/2]

CAMPBELL, ALLAN, Captain of the 42nd Highlanders, son of Campbell
of Barcaldine, at New York 22.5.1757, at Lake George, 1758,
Major 8.1762, received a land grant at Crown Point 1763, died
1795. [SRO.GD87.1/82-84][NYSHA.X]

CAMPBELL, ARCHIBALD, Lieutenant of the 42nd Highlanders in New
York 22.4.1757, wounded at Ticonderoga 7.1758.
[NYSHA.X][OBW24][SM.XX.437]

CAMPBELL, ARCHIBALD, Lieutenant of the 42nd Highlanders,
embarked for New York 11.1757. [NYSHA.X]

CAMPBELL, ARCHIBALD, Fredericksburg, New York, Captain of the
New York Company of Volunteers, died on Long Island.
[Pro. 8.1781 PCC]

CAMPBELL, General Sir ARCHIBALD, 71st Regiment in Georgia 1778-
1779.[SRO.NRAS.0028]

CAMPBELL, Colonel CHARLES, son of Patrick Campbell of Ardchattan, prisoner of the Americans in Dunstable 30 miles northwest of Boston, 1776-1780.[SRO.NRAS.0934.93-94]

CAMPBELL, COLIN, Ensign of the King's Orange Rangers 1776. [SRO.GD170.3436]

CAMPBELL, DONALD, Lieutenant of the 77th {Montgomery's Highlanders} Regiment wounded at Bushy Run 6.8.1763 [SM.XXV.575]

CAMPBELL, DONALD, Ensign of the 42nd Highlanders in New York 22.5.1757. [NYSHA.X]

CAMPBELL, DONALD, born 1754, Loyalist, British Army officer 1776-1783, died 18.8.1825. [Pro.31.8.1825 New York]

CAMPBELL, DUNCAN, of Inverawe, born 1703, Major of the 42nd Highlanders,died after Ticonderoga 17.7.1758.[SM.XX.437] [SRO GD87.1/84][NYSHA.X][Union Cemetery NY]

CAMPBELL, DUNCAN, Ensign of the 42nd Highlanders in New York 22.5 1757, wounded at Fort Pitt and at Bushy Run 6.8.1763. [NYSHA.X][SM.XXV.575]

CAMPBELL, GEORGE, Lieutenant of General Gage's Regiment, son of Patrick Campbell of Barcaldine, in New York 1759, allocated 5,000 acres in New York 4 1765.[SRO GD87 1/84][PCCol.IV.818]

CAMPBELL, GEORGE, Ensign of the 42nd Highlanders in New York 22.5 1757. [NYSHA.X]

CAMPBELL, HUGH, Lieutenant of the 35th Regiment, son of Duncan Campbell of Glenure, 1778. [SRO.GD170.1118/7-10]

CAMPBELL, JAMES, at Oswego 1755-1756. [SRO.NRAS.0029]

CAMPBELL, JAMES, Lieutenant of the 42nd Regiment in New York 22.5.1757. [NYSHA.X]

CAMPBELL, JAMES, surgeon's mate under General Braddock in America, son of Mrs Dorothy Campbell. [Pro. 6.1757 PCC]

CAMPBELL, JAMES, at Fort Prince George 310 miles north west of Charlestown 1761; in New Orleans 1764, in Arkansas, in Illinois 1767. [SRO.NRAS.0631 48/51/52/54]

CAMPBELL, JOHN, of Strachur, to America 6.1756, Captain of the 42nd Highlanders at New York 22.5.1757, wounded at Ticonderoga 1758, Lieutenant Colonel 2.1762; to Martinique and Havana 1763, to America 1776, Commander of British Forces in West Florida 1781, died 1806. [NYSHA.X][OBW27][SM.XX.437]

CAMPBELL, JOHN, of Duneavis, Perthshire, Captain of the 42nd Highlanders, to America 6.1756, in New York 22.5.1757, killed at Ticonderoga 1758. [NYSHA.X][OBW26][SM.XX.437]

CAMPBELL, JOHN, younger of Glenlyon, Lieutenant of the 42nd
Highlanders at New York 22.5.1757, wounded at Ticonderoga
1758. [NYSHA.X][OBW27][SM.XX.437]

CAMPBELL, Colonel MUNGO, in Staten Island 1777
[SRO.GD170.1166]; Colonel of the 52nd Regiment, killed at Fort
Montgomerie, North America. [TGSI.XXI.128]

CAMPBELL, Lieutenant 80th Light Infantry, killed at Niagara 14 9 1763
[SM.XXI.662]

CAMPBELL, PATRICK, son of Duncan Campbell of Glenure, Major of
the 71st Regiment in America 1776-1782. [SRO GD170 1176/10-
15; 1711/12-18]; died on Long Island 1782.
[SRO.GD170 1097/111]; husband of Sarah Pearsall, father of
Duncan. [SRO.GD170 1385/1-5]; [Pro. 6.1784 PCC]

CARMICHAEL, WILLIAM, private in the 42nd Highlanders {Captain
Reid's Company} in New York 10.1757. [CA.3 440]

CARR, DONALD, private in the 42nd Highlanders {Captain Reid's
Company} in New York 10.1757, killed in action. [CA.3.440]

CARR, JAMES, soldier of the 84th {Royal Highland Emigrant} Regiment
in New York 15 7.1778. [SRO.GD174.2120.3/4]

CARSON, ROBERT, Sergeant of the 22nd Foot who died in Mobile,
West Florida, son of Jane Irvine, wife of John Drummond.
[Pro. 4.1766 PCC]

CHISHOLM, ALEXANDER, emigrated from Fort William to America on
the Pearl 1773, settled on the Kingsborough Patent, New York,
Loyalist, soldier of the Royal Regiment of New York 1777-1783,
settled in Charlottenburg, Ontario. [DFpp]

CHISHOLM, ALEXANDER, in Glasgow, late of the 84th Regiment,
prisoner of the Americans 1778-. [SRO.GD174.2188]

CHISHOLM, WILLIAM, emigrated from Fort William to America on the
Pearl 1773, settled on the Kingsborough Patent, New York,
Loyalist, soldier of the Royal Regiment of New York, settled in
Charlottenburg, Ontario. [DFpp]

CHRISTIE, HUGH, private in the 42nd Highlanders {Captain Reid's
Company} in New York 10.1757 [CA.3 440]

CHRYSTIE, ROBERT PIGOT, Major in the 42nd Highlanders, died of
fever in St Lucia 23.6.1796. [OBW29]

CLARK, ROBERT, Lieutenant of the 18th Foot in Halifax, Nova Scotia.
[Cnf. 17.. Commisariat of Edinburgh]

CLARK, Sergeant, 42nd Highlanders, at Crown Point 6.9 1759
[NYSHA.X]

CLEPHANE, JAMES, Major of Colonel Simon Fraser's Highland Regiment, in Halifax, Connecticut, Fort Stanwix, and New York, 1757-1759. [SRO.GD125.box22]

COCKBURN, DOUGLAS, former Lieutenant in the South Carolina Regiment, resident in Edinburgh. [Cnf. 1793 Commissariat of Edinburgh]

COCKBURN, Sir JAMES, Lieutenant of the 42nd Highlanders in New York 22.5 1757 [NYSHA.X]

COCKBURN, WILLIAM, Captain of the 42nd Highlanders, killed in Martinique 1762. [OBW30]

COLQUHOUN, Captain WILLIAM, in America before 8.1777. [SRO GD248. box 54/5]

CONSTABLE, ALEXANDER, Lieutenant of the Fencible American Regiment, 28.8.1776. [SRO.RS27.228.161]

CRAMMOND, JAMES, Lieutenant of the 42nd Highlanders, wounded at Long Island 22.8.1776. [OBW31]

CUMMING, ALEXANDER, Sergeant of the 42nd Highlanders {Captain John Reid's Company} in New York 10.1757. [CA.3.440]

CUMMING, ALEXANDER, private in the 42nd Highlanders {Captain Reid's Company} in New York 10.1757. [CA.3.440]

CUMMING, JAMES, carpenter, 42nd Highlanders, at Ticonderoga 25 7.1759 [NYSHA.X]

CUMMING, JOHN, Corporal of the 42nd Highlanders {Captain John Reid's Company} in New York 10.1757 [CA.3 440]

CUNNINGHAME, ARCHIBALD, later of Cadel and Thornton, garrisoned at Louisbourg, Cape Breton Island, ca. 1748. [SRO.GD21.485]

CUTHBERT, JOHN, Lieutenant of Fraser's Highlanders, killed at Louisbourg 6.1758. [SM.XX.435][SHS.2.87]

DALGLEISH, JOHN, Lieutenant of the 21st {Royal Scots Fusiliers} Regiment, to America 1776, surrendered at Saratoga 17.10.1777. [RSF]

DALZELL, JAMES, second son of Sir Robert Dalzell of the Binns, Lieutenant of the 60th {Royal American} Regiment 1756, later of the 1st {Royal Scots} Regiment, killed at Fort Detroit 31.7.1763. [SM.XXV.572]

DAVISON, WILLIAM, probably from Peeblesshire, Captain of the 52nd Foot, who died in Boston. [Pro. 1776 PCC]

DICK, WILLIAM, Captain of an Independent Company of Foot in New York. [Cnf. 9.10.1747 Commissariat of Edinburgh]

DICKSON, DAVID, Hartree, Peeblesshire, former Captain of the 64th
Regiment of Foot, settled at Houma Chita on the River Missippi,
West Florida, before 1774. [PRO.CO5..613.257]

DONALDSON, JOHN, Lieutenant Colonel of the 55th Foot in New York,
Rogers and Albany, 1757-1758. [SRO GD45.2/26/1-5]

DOUGLAS, JOHN, at Fort Stanwix 1758. [SRO.NRAS.0859 70]

DOUGLAS, STUART, Lieutenant Colonel, granted 10,000 acres in East
Florida 5.1764. [PC Col.IV.813]

DOUGLAS, WILLIAM, Lieutenant of the 21st {Royal Scots Fusiliers}
Regiment, to America 1776, surrendered at Saratoga 17 10 1777
[RSF]

DUNBAR, JAMES, Captain of the 3rd Battalion, Royal Regiment of
Artillery, died in New York. [Pro. 10 1783 PCC]

DUNBAR, THOMAS, Major General, in Bedford, Long Island, and in
Philadelphia 1778. [SRO.NRAS.0065.6]

DUNDAS, Lieutenant RALPH, allocated 10,000 acres in Cape Breton,
1767 [PC Col.V.598]

EDDINGTON, JAMES, former officer of the 42nd Highlanders, allocated
a land grant of 2,000 acres on west side of the Connecticut River,
Cumberland County, New York, 22.10.1766. [NY Col. MS.7 904]

ELLIOT, ANDREW, Major of the Royal Marines, died in Rhode Island,
son of Mrs Katherine Elliot. [Pro. 9 1778 PCC]

FARMER, JASPER, Captain of the 21st {Royal Scots Fusiliers}
Regiment, to America 1776, surrendered at Saratoga 17.10 1777
[RSF]

FARQUHARSON, ALEXANDER, Ensign of the 42nd Highlanders,
embarked for America 11.1757, Captain 1758, died in Havanna
1762.[NYSHA.X][OBW37]

FARQUHARSON, GEORGE, Lieutenant of the 42nd Highlanders in New
York 22.5 1757, killed at Ticonderoga 7.1758.
[NYSHA.X][OBW37][SM.XX.437]

FARQUHARSON, JAMES, private in the 42nd Highlanders {Captain
Reid's Company} in New York 10.1757, killed in action.
[CA.3.440]

FEATHERSTONE, WILLIAM, Lieutenant of the 21st {Royal Scots
Fusiliers} Regiment, to America 1776, surrendered at Saratoga
17.10.1777. [RSF]

FENWICK, ROBERT, Captain Lieutenant of the Royal Regiment of
Artillery, who died in New York. [Pro. 1.1786 PCC]

FERGUSON, PATRICK, Major of the 71st Regiment, died in Carolina.
Pro. 8.1782 PCC [SRO.NRAS.0783.28/29]

FINNIE, WILLIAM, possibly from Aberdeen, Lieutenant of 61st
Company, 2nd Division of Marines, who died in Boston.
[Pro. 11.1775 PCC]

FLETCHER, ALEXANDER, former Captain of the 84th {Royal Highland
Emigrant} Regiment, settled in Prince Edward Island after 1783,
died in St Johns 1793 [SM.55.619]

FORBES, ALEXANDER, mason. 42nd Highlanders, at Crown Point
5 9 1759. [NYSHA.X]

FORBES, ARTHUR, born 1753, soldier in the North Carolina
Highlanders, died in Stirling 1831. [Stirling g/s]

FORBES, JOHN, private in the 42nd Highlanders {Captain Reid's
Company} in New York 10.1757. [CA.3.440]

FORBES, JOHN, Brigadier General, to Ohio and and capture of Fort
Duquesne 1759, died in Philadelphia 1759.
[SRO.RH15.38/81-83-120-140-145]

FORBES, Captain WILLIAM, in Schenectady 1757-1758.
[SRO.GD21.2/30/1-3]

FORDYCE, CHARLES, possibly from Edinburgh, Captain of the 14th
Foot, who died in Virginia. [Pro. 6.1775 PCC]

FORSTER, GEORGE, Major of the 21st {Royal Scots Fusiliers}
Regiment, to America 1776, surrendered at Saratoga 17.10 1777
[RSF]

FRASER, ALEXANDER, Lieutenant of Fraser's Highlanders, killed at
Louisbourg 6.1758. [SHS.2.87]

FRASER, ALEXANDER, former Lieutenant of the 78th {Fraser
Highlanders} Regiment, received a land grant in New York 1773.
[PCCol.5.597]

FRASER, ALEXANDER, Lieutenant and Adjutant of the 71st Regiment,
who died in Savannah, Georgia. [Pro. 12.1783 PCC]

FRASER, ALEXANDER, private of the 42nd Highlanders {Captain
Reid's Company} in New York 10.1757. [CA.3.440]

FRASER, DONALD, private in the 42nd Highlanders {Captain Reid's
Cpompany} in New York 10.1757. [CA.3.440]

FRASER, DONALD, private in the 42nd Highlanders {Captain Reid's
Company} in New York 10.1757. [CA.3.440]

FRASER, HUGH, former Captain in the 78th {Fraser Highlanders}
Regiment, received a land grant in New York 26.8.1773
[PCCol.5.597]

FRASER, HUGH, private in the 42nd Highlanders {Captain Reid's
Company} in New York 10.1757. [CA.3.440]

FRASER, HUGH, private in the 42nd Highlanders {Captain Reid's
Company} in New York 10.1757, killed in action. [CA.3.440]

FRASER, JAMES, born in Inverness 1739, labourer, deserted from the
22nd Regiment of Foot in New York 4.1761
[New York Mercury, 11.5.1761]

FRASER, JAMES, born in Scotland 1751, soldier in the 2nd Battalion
Royal Highlanders in Philadelphia 20.5.1778, in New York
15.7.1778. [SRO.GD174.2120.2/3]

FRASER, JAMES, carpenter of the 42nd Highlanders, at Ticonderoga
25.7 1759. [NYSHA.X]

FRASER, JOHN, soldier 42nd Highlanders, at Crown Point 27.8.1759
[NYSHA.X]

FRASER, JOHN, former Captain of the 78th [Fraser Highlanders]
Regiment, received a land grant in New York 26.8.1773
[PCCol.5.597]

FRASER, MALCOLM, Captain of the 84th [Royal Highland Emigrant]
Regiment in Canada 1778. [SRO.GD174.2123]

FRASER, SIMON, of Inverallochy, Captain of 78th [Fraser's
Highlanders], killed at the Heights of Abraham, Quebec, 1759.
[SHS.2.87]

FRASER, SIMON, Lieutenant Colonel of the 78th Foot at Fairfield and
Stratford, 1757-1758. [SRO.GD21.2/29/1-5]; land grant in Albany
County, New York, 1773. [PC.Col.V.598]

FRASER, THOMAS, Captain of the 14th Regiment, who died in Norfolk,
Virginia, son of Simon Fraser of Finallan. [Pro. 1 1790 PCC]

FRASER, ........, sergeant of the 78th Foot at Fairfield and Stratford, 1757-
1758.[SRO.GD21.2/29/1-5]

FRASER, WILLIAM, Corporal of the 2nd Battalion Royal Highlanders
under Captain Murdoch MacLaine in America 2.5 1778.
[SRO.GD174.2120.2]

FRASER, ......, Lieutenant, 80th Light Infantry, killed at Niagara
14.9.1763. [SM.XXV.685]

FRASER, ..... Lieutenant of the 78th [Fraser's Highlanders], killed at
Louisbourg 6.1758.[SM.XX.435]

GAMBLE, GEORGE, soldier of the 84th [Royal Highland
Emigrant] Regiment in New York 1778. [SRO GD174.2120 4]

GORDON, Major A., commanding officer of the 26th Regiment in New
York 1777. [SRO.NRAS.0696.2]

GORDON, COSMO, Lieutenant of the 78th [Fraser's Highlanders]
Regiment, killed in Quebec 1760. [SHS.2.87]

GORDON, HENRY, Captain of Engineers, allocated 5,000 acres in New
York 5.1765. [PC Col.IV.819]

GORDON, Lieutenant HUGH 1759. [SRO GD297.404]

GORDON, JAMES, Colonel of the 80th Regiment, who died in New York, son of Mrs Elizabeth Gordon. [Pro. 5.1784 PCC]

GORDON, JAMES, private of the 42nd Highlanders {Captain Reid's Company} in New York 10.1757. [CA.3.441]

GORDON, PETER, Captain, allocated 5,000 acres in New York 5.1765. [PC Col.IV.819]

GORDON, WILLIAM BRACO, at Charles Town Heights, Massachusetts, 1775 [SRO.NRAS.0920.27]

GORDON, WILLIAM, private of the 42nd Highlanders {Captain Reid's Company} in New York 10.1757. [CA.3.441]

GRAEME, DAVID, of Braco, Major General, allocated a grant of Hasenclaver Patent, New York, 27.2.1769. [NY Book of Patents. XIV.314]

GRAEME, JOHN, Lieutenant of the 42nd Highlanders, wounded at Ticonderoga 1758, Captain when wounded at Fort Pitt 1763 [OBW43]

GRAEME, PATRICK, of Inchbraco, Lieutenant of the 42nd Highlanders, wounded at Fort Washington 1776, died 22.10.1781. [OBW43]

GRAEME, THOMAS, of Duchray, to America 1756,Captain of the 42nd Highlanders, at New York 22.5.1757, wounded at Ticonderoga 7 1758, wounded at Bushy Run 1763, allocated 5,000 acres in New York 3.1765. [NYSHA.X][OBW43][PC Col.IV.818][SM.XX.437]

GRAHAM, CHARLES, son of Graham of Drainie, officer of the 42nd Highlanders 1760-1798, wounded in St Vincent 1796. [OBW43]

GRAHAM, GORDON, of Drainie, to America 1756, Captain of the 42nd Highlanders in New York 22.5.1757, at Fort William Henry 1757,wounded at Ticonderoga 7.1758, to Martinique 1762, to Fort Pitt 1763, at Battle of Bushy Run. [NYSHA.X] [OBW43] [SM.XX.437]

GRAHAM, JOHN, Lieutenant and quartermaster of the 42nd Highlanders in New York 22.5.1757, wounded at Ticonderoga 7.1758, also at Bushy Run 1763 and at Fort Pitt 1763. [NYSHA.X][OBW43][SM.XX.437][SM.XXV.575]

GRAHAM, JOHN, Captain of the 42nd Highlanders, killed at Fort Pitt 1763. [OBW43][SM.XXV.575]

GRAHAM, JOHN, private in the 42nd Highlanders {Captain Reid's Company} in New York 10.1757. [CA.3.440]

GRANT, ALEXANDER, Sergeant of the 2nd Battalion, 42nd {Royal Highland} Regiment under Lord John Murray, who died in Havanna, husband of Barbara Grant in New York. [Pro. 1766 PCC]

GRANT, ALEXANDER, born in Glen Moriston 1733, to America as a Lieutenant of a Highland Regiment in 1754. Member of H.M. Executive and Legislative Council of Upper Canada. Died on his estate of Gross Point near Detroit 1813. [Edinburgh Advertiser,5197.13]

GRANT, ALEXANDER, officer of the 42nd Highlanders, wounded at Fort Washington 16.11.1776, wounded at Yorktown 12.5 1781, died 1807. [OBW44]

GRANT, ANGUS, emigrated to America 1774, settled on the Kingsborough Patent, New York, Loyalist, soldier of the Royal Regiment of New York, settled in Charlottenburg, Ontario. [DFpp]

GRANT, ARCHIBALD, emigrated to America 1774, settled on the Kingsborough Patent, New York, Loyalist, soldier in the Royal Regiment of New York 1776-1783, settled in Charlottenburg, Ontario. [DFpp]

GRANT, DONALD, private in the 42nd Highlanders {Captain Reid's Company} in New York 10 1757. [CA.3 440]

GRANT, DONALD, emigrated from Fort William to America on the Pearl 1773, settled on the Kingsborough Patent, New York, Loyalist, soldier of the Royal Regiment of New York 1776-1783, settled in Charlottenburg, Ontario. [DFpp]

GRANT, DONALD, weaver in Croskey, emigrated from Fort William to America on the Pearl 1773, settled on the Kingsborough Patent, New York, Loyalist, soldier of the Royal Regiment of New York 1776-1783, settled in Charlottenburg, Ontario. [DFpp]

GRANT, DUNCAN, 21st Regiment in America 1777. [SRO.GD248. box 509/3]

GRANT, DUNCAN, emigrated from Fort William to America on the Pearl 1773, settled on the Kingsborough Patent, New York, Loyalist, soldier of the Royal Regiment of New York 1776-1783, settled in Charlottenburg, Ontario. [DFpp]

GRANT, FINLAY, emigrated from Fort William to America on the Pearl 1773, settled on the Kingsborough Patent, New York, Loyalist, soldier of the Royal Regiment of New York, settled in Charlottenburg, Ontario. [DFpp]

GRANT, FRANCIS, to America 1756, Lieutenant Colonel of the 42nd Highlanders, wounded at Ticonderoga, at New York 22.5 1757, to Oswego and Montreal 1760, Colonel of the 90th Light Infantry 1762, to Martinique and Havana1762, died 1782. [NYSHA.X]

GRANT, JAMES, of Ballindalloch, Major of the 77th Foot, to Fort Duquesne 8.1758.[SRO.GD21.2/61/1-2]

GRANT, JAMES, Lieutenant of the 42nd Highlanders at New York
22.5.1757, adjutant, wounded at Ticonderoga 7.1758, died 1778.
[SM.XX.437][NYSHA.X][OBW45]

GRANT, JAMES, private in the 42nd Highlanders {Captain Reid's
Company} in New York 10.1757. [CA.3.440]

GRANT, JOHN, private in the 42nd Highlanders {Captain Reid's
Company} in New York 10.1757 [CA.3 441]

GRANT, JOHN, private in the 42nd Highlanders {Captain Reid's
Company} in New York 10.1757. [CA.3.441]

GRANT, JOHN, Lieutenant of the 42nd Highlanders, served in Albany,
Oswego, Montreal, etc. 1759-1761, embarked at Staten Island
12.1761. [SRO.RH4.77]

GRANT, JOHN, emigrated from Fort William to America on the Pearl
1773, settled on the Kingsborough Patent, New York, Loyalist,
soldier of the Royal Regiment of New York, died in Canada 1777
[DFpp]

GRANT, Captain JOHN, Commissary General and Paymaster of
Ordnance in America, died 1780. [SRO.GD248.box 227-235-244]

GRANT, JONATHAN, Corporal of the 42nd Highlanders {Captain John
Reid's Company} in New York 10.1757 [CA.3 440]

GRANT, NEIL, New York, Lieutenant of the 77th Foot, husband of Helen
Grant. [Pro. 8.1763 PCC]

GRANT, PETER, Ensign of the 42nd Highlanders in New York
22.5 1757, wounded at Ticonderoga 7.1758.
[NYSHA.X][OBW45][SM.XX.437]

GRANT, PETER, emigrated to America 1774, settled on the
Kingsborough Patent, New York, Loyalist, soldier of the Royal
Regiment of New York 1776-1783, settled in Charlottenburg,
Ontario. [DFpp]

GRANT, Captain ROBERT, at Amboy 6.1777, in Maryland 10.1777.
[SRO.GD248.box 509/3; box 55/1]

GRANT, WILLIAM, Captain of the 42nd Highlanders at New York
22.5 1757, wounded at Ticonderoga 7.1758. [NYSHA.X][OBW45]

GRANT, WILLIAM, Lieutenant of the 42nd Highlanders, wounded at
Ticonderoga 7 1758, died in Havanna 1762.
[OBW45][SM.XX.437]

GRANT, WILLIAM, private of the 42nd Highlanders {Captain Reid's
Company} in New York 10.1757. [CA.3.441]

GRANT, ..., Lieutenant of the 42nd Highlanders, wounded in South
Carolina 1780. [SM.XXXXII.265]

GRANT, ...Major of Highlanders, killed at Fort DuQuesne 14.9.1758.
[SM.XX.548]

GRAY, JAMES, Lieutenant of the 42nd Highlanders in New York
22.5.1757.[NYSHA.X]

GRAY, ROBERT, Lieutenant of the 42nd Highlanders at New York
22.5.1757, wounded at Ticonderoga 7.1758, died 1771
[NYSHA.X][SM.XX.437]

GRIERSON, JAMES, settled in Georgia, Loyalist Militia Captain 1773,
died in Georgia. [PRO.AO13.35.247/258]

GULLINE, WILLIAM, probably from Stranraer, Lieutenant of a New
York Independent Company of Foot, who died in Havanna.
[Pro. 12.1763 PCC]

HALDANE, DAVID, Captain of the 42nd Highlanders, allocated 5,000
acres in New York 4.1765 [PC Col.IV.818]

HALYBURTON, Reverend WILLIAM, chaplain to the 2nd Battalion, 1st
{Royal Scots} Regiment, allocated 5,000 acres in New York
8.1765. [PC Col.IV.819]

HAMILTON, ARCHIBALD, Captain of the 56th regiment, allocated
5,000 acres in New York 4.1765 [PC Col.IV.818]

HAMILTON, HUGH, Pensacola, Lieutenant of H.M. Forces.
[Pro. 4.1793 PCC]

HAMILTON, JAMES, Brigadier General, 21st {Royal Scots Fusiliers}
Regiment, to America 1776, surrendered at Saratoga 17.10.1777
[RSF]

HAMILTON, WILLIAM, Captain in the Royal North Carolina Regiment,
prisoner of the Americans 1781. [SRO.NRAS.0620.5]

HENDERSON, JAMES, Lieutenant of the 78th Regiment, died in New
York, husband of Elizabeth Henderson in New York.
[Pro. 10.1770 PCC]

HENDERSON, JAMES, late of Jedburgh, resident in New York, surgeon
to the Royal Artillery, 1778. [SRO.GD53.198]; died in New York.
[Pro. 4.1781 PCC]

HENDERSON, JOHN, born 1709, "at the battles of Culloden and
Minden, and at the taking of Quebec after which he settled in
America". Died in Fishkill, America, 13.12.1811 [SM.74.316]

HENDERSON, THOMAS, surgeon of the 90th Regiment, died in
Havanna 7.1762. [Skirling g/s]

HEPBURN, JOHN, Lieutenant of the 21st {Royal Scots Fusiliers}
Regiment, to America 1776, surrendered at Saratoga 17.10.1777.
[RSF]

HOME, JAMES, officer of the Royal Marines in the West Indies, 1778-
1782.[SRO.GD1.384/6-7]

HOME, WILLIAM, officer of the Royal Marines in the West Indies,
1778-1782. [SRO.GD1.384/6-7]

HOOD, HUGH, born in Scotland 1744, soldier of the 2nd Battalion Royal
    Highlanders in Philadelphia 20.5 1778. [SRO.GD174.2120.2]
HOUSTON, PATRICK, Quartermaster of General Oglethorpe's Regiment
    in Georgia, 1748. [SRO.GD18.5360.9]
INNES, Captain ROBERT, in Quebec 7.1777 [SRO.GD248.box 54/4]
    [SRO.NRAS.1100.8]
INNES, ROBERT, Lieutenant of the 21st {Royal Scots Fusiliers}
    Regiment, to America 1776, surrendered at Saratoga 17.10.1777.
    [RSF]
JACK, GEORGE, soldier of the 84th {Royal Highland Emigrant}
    Regiment in New York 15 7.1778. [SRO.GD174.2120.3/4]
JOHNSTON, FRANCIS, Lieutenant of 38th Regiment, died in
    Philadelphia. [Pro. 12.1778 PCC]
KEIR, Captain Lieutenant GEORGE, at New York 1778, at Savannah,
    Georgia, 7.1779. [SRO.NRAS.0631 79/81]
KENNEDY, DONALD, private of the 42nd Highlanders {Captain Reid's
    Company} in New York 10 1757 [CA.3 441]
KENNEDY, DONALD, private of the 42nd Highlanders {Captain Reid's
    Company} in New York 10.1757 [CA.3.441]
KENNEDY, JOHN, private of the 42nd Highlanders {Captain Reid's
    Company} in New York 10 1757 [CA.3 441]
KENNEDY, ROBERT, sawyer, 42nd Highlanders, at Crown Point,
    16.8.1759 [NYSHA.X]
KIRKMAN, THOMAS MICHAEL, Captain of the 21st {Royal Scots
    Fusiliers} Regiment, to America 1776, surrendered at Saratoga
    17 10 1777. [RSF]
LAPSLEY, Lieutenant, died in Havanna 1762. [OBW54]
LESLIE, ALEXANDER, Major General, in America 1773-1782.
    [SRO GD26.9/512/5-21, 9/518]
LESLIE, GEORGE, Lieutenant of the 42nd Highlanders 1758, wounded
    at Guadaloupe, and in Martinique 1759 and 1762. [OBW55]
LESLIE, WILLIAM, second son of the Earl of Leven, Captain of the 17th
    Regiment, in Long Island, etc. 1771-1777, killed at the Battle of
    Princeton. [SRO.GD26.9/513; GD26.13.678]
LIVINGSTONE, WILLIAM, of Bodlonne, Linlithgow, formerly
    Lieutenant on half pay of an Independent Company of Foot in
    Carolina. [Pro. 6.1770 PCC]
LOVELL, JAMES, Captain of the 21st {Royal Scots Fusiliers} Regiment,
    to America 1776, surrendered at Saratoga 17 10.1777. [RSF]
LYON, GEORGE, formerly of Cape Fear, North Carolina, Colonel of the
    Royal North Carolina Regiment. [Pro. 8.1790 PCC]

MCADAM, Captain GILBERT, in Boston, New York and Greenwich 1758. [SRO GD21.2/68/1,3, 5-7]

MCADAM, GEORGE, private of the 42nd Highlanders [Captain Reid's Company] in New York 10.1757 [CA.3.441]

MCANDREW, JOHN, Sergeant in the 42nd Highlanders [Captain John Reid's Company] in New York 10 1757. [CA.3 440]

MCARTHUR, DUNCAN, soldier of the 2nd Battalion Royal Highlanders in America 2.5 1778. [SRO.GD174.2120.2]

MCARTHUR, ARTHUR, Major of the 71st Regiment 1780 [SRO.NRAS.0934.94]

MCARTHUR, DUNCAN, soldier of the 2nd Battalion, 84th [Royal Highland Emigrant] Regiment in New York 15 7 1778 [SRO GD174.2120.3]

MCARTHUR, DUNCAN, tailor of the 84th Regiment 1781 [SRO.GD174.2159]

MCARTHUR, JOHN, private of the 42nd Highlanders [Captain Reid's Company] in New York 10 1757 [CA.3.441]

MCARTHUR, Major PATRICK, at Broad River, South Carolina, 1780 [SRO.NRAS.0783.29]

MCBEAN, DONALD, former Captain of the 78th [Fraser Highlanders] received a land grant in New York 1773 [PCCol 5.597]

MCCASKILL, JOHN, born 1758, soldier of the 45th Regiment, died in battle in the West Indies 6.6.1796. [Eynort, Skye, g/s]

MCCLOUD, JOHN, New York, Sergeant of the 42nd Regiment. [Pro. 3 1765 PCC]

MCCOLL, DONALD, private of the 42nd Highlanders [Captain Reid's Company] in New York 10 1757 [CA.3.441]

MCCOLME, JOHN, carpenter, 42nd Highlanders, at Ticonderoga 25.7.1759. [NYHA.X]

MCDIARMID, DONALD, private of the 42nd Highlanders [Captain Reid's Company] in New York 10.1757 [CA.3 441]

MCDONALD, ALEXANDER, soldier of the 2nd Battalion, 84th [Royal Highland Regiment] in New York 15.7 1778. [SRO GD174.2120.3]

MCDONALD, Captain ALEXANDER, paymaster of the 2nd Battalion, Royal Highland Emigrants, 1778, at Fort Edward and Halifax 1778-1784. [SRO GD174.2124-2126]

MACDONALD, ALEXANDER, of Kingsburgh, late Captain of North Carolina Volunteers, husband of Annabella Macdonald at Mugstole, Skye. [Pro. 5.1798 PCC]

MCDONALD, ALEXANDER, in Aberdeen, late Captain of the Florida Rangers. [Pro. 4 1805 PCC]

MCDONALD, ALLAN, soldier of the 84th {Royal Highland Emigrant} Regiment in New York 1778. [SRO.GD174.2120.4]

MACDONALD, Lieutenant ALLAN, in Long Island 1781-1782. [SRO.NRAS.0139 1]

MCDONALD, ANGUS, Corporal of the 42nd Highlanders {Captain John Reid's Company} in New York 10.1757. [CA.3.440]

MCDONALD, ANGUS, private of the 42nd Highlanders {Captain Reid's Company} in New York 10.1757 [CA.3.441]

MCDONALD, ANGUS, mason, 42nd Highlanders, at Crown Point 17 8.1759. [NYSHA.X]

MCDONALD, ANGUS, soldier of the 2nd Battalion, 84th {Royal Highland Emigrant} Regiment in New York 15 7 1778. [SRO GD174.2120.3]

MCDONALD, ARCHIBALD, private of the 42nd Highlanders {Captain Reid's Company} in New York 10 1757. [CA.3 441]

MCDONALD, ARCHIBALD, private of the 42nd Highlanders {Captain Reid's Company} in New York 10 1757, later killed in action. [CA.3 441]

MCDONALD, ARCHIBALD, soldier of the 2nd Battalion, 84th {Royal Highland Emigrant}Regiment in New York 15.7 1778. [SRO GD174.2120.3]

MCDONALD, DONALD, Captain of Fraser's Highlanders, wounded at Louisbourg 6 1758. [SM.XX.435]; killed at Quebec 1760. [SHS.2.87]

MACDONALD, DONALD, former merchant in Edinburgh, and former Lieutenant of the 105th Foot, died at Cross Creek, North Carolina, 1 1773 [SM.35.223]

MCDONALD, DONALD, late Lieutenant Colonel of the American Provincials, late in Edinburgh, husband of Jane McDonald. [Pro. 5 1789 PCC]

MCDONALD, GEORGE, soldier of the 2nd Battalion, 84th {Royal Highland Emigrant} Regiment in New York 15 7.1778. [SRO GD174.2120.3]

MCDONALD, HUGH, soldier of the 2nd Battalion, 84th {Royal Highland Emigrant} Regiment in New York 15.7 1778. [SRO.GD174.2120.3]

MCDONALD, JAMES, volunteer in the 84th {Royal Highland Emigrant} Regiment in New York 15.7.1778. [SRO GD174.2120.3]

MCDONALD, JAMES, private of the 42nd Highlanders {Captain Reid's Company} in New York 10 1757, killed in action. [CA.3 441]

MCDONALD, JAMES, carpenter, 42nd Highlanders, at Ticonderoga 25 7 1759 [NYSHA.X]

MCDONALD, JOHN, private of the 42nd Highlanders {Captain Reid's Company} in New York 10.1757. [CA.3 441]

MCDONALD, JOHN, Lieutenant of Fraser's Highlanders, wounded at Louisbourg 6.1758. [SM.XX.435]

MCDONALD, JOHN Ensign of Highlanders, killed at Fort DuQuesne 14.9.1758. [SM.XX.548]

MCDONALD, JOHN, soldier of the 84th {Royal Highland Emigrant} Regiment in New York 1778. [SRO.GD174.2120 4]

MCDONALD, LACHLAN, private in the 42nd Highlanders {Captain Reid's Company} in New York 10.1757. [CA.3 441]

MACDONALD, LAUGHLIN, born before 1721, soldier in Loudoun's Highland Regiment under Wolfe at Quebec, died in Belfast, USA, 25.8.1821 [DPCA

MCDONALD, WILLIAM, late Captain of the 79th Foot, then Lieutenant Governor of Fort Augusta, Jamaica. Cnf. 21 12.1791 Edinburgh

MCDONALD, ..., Captain of Highlanders, killed at Fort Duquesne 14.9.1758. [SM.XX.548]

MACDONNELL, AENEAS, former Captain of the 6th Royal Veteran Regiment, died in Nelson, Miramachi, New Brunswick, 10.3 1828. [BM.24.807]

MCDONELL, ALEXANDER, son of McDonell of Barrisdale, killed on the Heights of Abraham, Quebec, 1760. [SHS.2.87]

MCDONELL, ALEXANDER, born in Boleskin, Stratherrick, emigrated to America 1773, settled on the Kingsborough Patent, New York, Loyalist, soldier in the 1st Battalion of the Royal Regiment of New York 1776-1783, settled at River aux Raisin, Ontario. [DFpp]

MCDONELL, ALEXANDER, born in Knoydart, emigrated to America 1773, settled on the Kingsborough Patent, New York, Loyalist, soldier in the 84th {Royal Highland Emigrant} Regiment, settled in Cornwall, Ontario. [DFpp]

MCDONELL, ALEXANDER, born in Aberchalder, Jacobite 1745, emigrated to America on the Pearl from Fort William 1773, settled on the Kingsborough Patent, New York, Loyalist, Captain of the 84th {Royal Highland Emigrant} Regiment and later of the Royal Regiment of New York, settled in Glengarry, Canada. [DFpp]

MCDONELL, ALEXANDER, born in Fort Augustus 1762, son of Allan McDonell and Helen Chisholm, emigrated from Fort William to America on the Pearl 1773, Loyalist, soldier of the 84th {Royal Highland Emigrant} Regiment and later of Butler's Rangers, settled in Canada, died in Toronto 1842. [DFpp]

MCDONELL, ALLAN, born in Collachie, Loch Oich, 1712, Jacobite in 1745, emigrated from Fort William to America on the Pearl 1773, settled on the Kingsborough Patent, New York, Loyalist, Captain of the 84th {Royal Highland Emigrant} Regiment, settled in Quebec 1779, married Helen McNab, died at Cap Rouge, Quebec, 1792. [DFpp]

MCDONELL, ALLAN, emigrated from Fort William to America on the Pearl 1773, settled on the Kingsborough Patent, New York, Loyalist, soldier of the 1st Battalion of the Royal Regiment of New York, settled in Charlottenburg, Ontario. [DFpp]

MCDONELL, ANGUS, emigrated from Fort Wiliam to America on the Pearl 1773, settled on the Kingsborough Patent, New York, Loyalist, soldier of the 84th {Royal Highland Emigrant} Regiment, settled in Cornwall, Ontario. [DFpp]

MCDONELL, ARCHIBALD, emigrated from Fort William to America on the Pearl 1773, settled on the Kingsborough Patent, New York, Loyalist, Lieutenant of the 84th {Royal Highland Emigrant} Regiment. [DFpp]

MACDONELL, CHARLES, from Glen Garry, Lieutenant of Fraser's Highlanders, killed at St Johns. [SHS.2.87]

MCDONELL, DONALD, born in Kilmorack, emigrated from Fort William to America on the Pearl 1773, settled on the Kingsborough Patent, New York, Loyalist, Corporal of the 84th {Royal Highland Emigrant} Regiment, settled in Charlottenburg, Ontario. [DFpp]

MACDONNELL, JOHN, Major of the 78th {Fraser Highlanders} Regiment, received a land grant in New York 1773. [PCCol.5.597]

MCDOUGALL, GEORGE, carpenter, 42nd Highlanders, at Ticonderoga 25 7 1759. [NYSHA.X]

MCEACHERN, NEIL, private in the 42nd Highlanders {Captain Reid's Company} in New York 10.1757 [CA.3.441]

MCELVORE, JOHN, soldier, 42nd Highlanders, at Crown Point 27.8.1759 [NYSHA.X]

MCFARLANE, JOHN, sawyer, 42nd Highlanders, at Crown Point, 16 8 1759 [NYSHA.X]

MCFARLANE, PETER, private in the 42nd Highlanders {Captain Reid's Company} in New York 10.1757, killed in action. [CA.3.441]

MCGILLEVRAY, JOHN, private in the 42nd Highlanders {Captain Reid's Company} in New York 10.1757. [CA.3.441]

MCGILLIVRAY, Lieutenant Colonel JOHN, Georgia 1789. [SRO.RS.Ross & Cromarty, 74]

MCGLASHAN, LEONARD, private in the 42nd Highlanders {Captain Reid's Company} in New York 10.1757 [CA.3 441]

MCGREGOR, ALEXANDER, private of the 42nd Highlanders {Captain Reid's Company} in New York 10 1757 [CA.3 441]

MCGREGOR, DONALD, private of the 42nd Highlanders {Captain Reid's Company} in New York 10.1757. [CA.3 441]

MCGREGOR, ROBERT, private of the 42nd Highlanders {Captain Reid's Company} in New York 10 1757. [CA.3.441]

MCGREGOR, ..., Ensign of the 71st Regiment, killed in South Carolina 1780 [SM.XXXXII.265]

MCGREGOR, WILLIAM, private of the 1st Battalion, Royal Highland Regiment, died in Havanna, husband of Mary McGregor in New York. [Pro. 3 1766 PCC]

MCINTOSH, ALEXANDER, Lieutenant of the 42nd Highlanders at New York 22.5 1757, wounded at Ticonderoga 7 1758, killed at Fort Washington 16.11.1776 [NYSHA.X][OBW60][SM.XX.437]

MCINTOSH, ALEXANDER, Ensign of the 42nd Highlanders in New York 22.5.1757, wounded in Martinique. [NYSHA.X]

MACKINTOSH, ANGUS, of Kellachy, Captain of Fraser's Highlanders, former Captain of the Keith Highlanders, died in South Carolina 1780 [SHS.2.112]

MACINTOSH, GREGOR, Sergeant of the 42nd Regiment, who died at Havanna, husband of Catherine MacIntosh in New York [Pro. 6.1765 PCC]

MCINTOSH, JAMES, Ensign of the 42nd Highlanders in New York 22.5 1757, wounded at Fort Pitt. [NYSHA.X]

MCINTOSH, JOHN, private of the 42nd Highlanders {Captain Reid's Company} in New York 10 1757. [CA.3 441]

MACKINTOSH, JOHN, Lieutenant of the 42nd Highlanders 1776, wounded at York Island. [OBW61]

MCINTYRE, ALEXANDER, private in the 42nd Highlanders {Captain Reid's Company} in New York 10.1757 [CA.3 441]

MCINTYRE, DONALD, private in the 42nd Highlanders {Captain Reid's Company} in New York 10.1757. [CA.3 441]

MCINTYRE, JAMES, private in the 42nd Highlanders {Captain Reid's Company} in New York 10 1757, killed in action. [CA.3 441]

MCINTYRE, PETER, soldier of the 2nd Battalion Royal Highland Regiment in Philadelphia 20.5.1778, in New York 15 7 1778. [SRO.GD174.2120.2/3]

MCINTYRE, WALTER, drummer of the 42nd Highlanders {Captain John Reid's Company} in New York 10.1757, later killed in action. [CA.3.440]

MCINVEN, HECTOR, private in the 42nd Highlanders {Captain Reid's Company} in New York 10 1757 [CA.3 441]

MACKAY, ALEXANDER, Lieutenant of the 42nd Highlanders embarked for America 11 1757. [NYSHA.X]

MCKAY, HUGH, private of the 42nd Highlanders {Captain Reid's Company} in New York 10.1757. [CA.3.441]

MCKAY, JOHN, soldier in the 2nd Battalion, 84th {Royal Highland Emigrant} Regiment in New York 15.7.1778. [SRO GD174.2120.3]

MACKAY, ROBERT, Lieutenant of the 88th Foot, who died in Virginia, son of Jean Mackay in Rothesay. [Pro. 9.1772 PCC]

MACKAY, WILLIAM, son of Hugh Mackay of Coylstrome, Captain of the Queens Rangers 1776-1783, settled at Bay of Quinte, Lake Ontario, 1785 [BOM]

MCKEAFTER, DOUGAL, mason, 42nd Highlanders, at Crown Point 16.8.1759. [NYSHA.X]

MCKENZIE, A., Lieutenant of Highlanders, killed at Fort DuQuesne 14 9 1758. [SM.XX.548]

MCKENZIE, ALEXANDER, private in the 42nd Highlanders {Captain Reid's Company} in New York 10.1757. [CA.3.441]

MACKENZIE, ALEXANDER, private of the 42nd Royal Highland Regiment, who died in Havanna, husband of Margaret McKenzie in New York. [Pro 3 1766 PCC]

MACKENZIE, ALEXANDER, Ensign of the 42nd Highlanders 1761 and 1773, died of wounds at York Island 17.9.1776 [OBW59]

MCKENZIE, DAVID, Lieutenant of the Royal American Regiment, son of David Mackenzie, shipmaster in Inverness. [Cnf. 11 1 1776 Commisariat of Edinburgh]

MCKENZIE, HUGH, private of the 42nd Highlanders {Captain Reid's Company} in New York 10.1757. [CA.3.441]

MCKENZIE, HUGH, private of the 42nd Highlanders {Captain Reid's Company} in New York 10.1757. [CA.3.441]

MCKENZIE, HUGH, Captain of Highlanders, killed at Fort DuQuesne 14 9 1758. [SM.XX.548]

MCKENZIE, JOHN, private of the 42nd Highlanders {Captain Reid's Company} in New York 10.1757, killed in action. [CA.3 441]

MCKENZIE, JOHN, private of the 42nd Highlanders {Captain Reid's Company} in New York 10.1757. [CA.3.441]

MCKENZIE, JOHN, soldier of the 2nd Battalion, 84th {Royal Highland Emigrant} Regiment in New York 15.7.1778. [SRO.GD174.2120.3]

MACKENZIE, ROBERT, Corporal of the 77th Regiment, who died in Amboy.[Pro. 5 1764 PCC]

MCKENZIE, RODERICK, private of the 42nd Highlanders {Captain
Reid's Company} in New York 10.1757 [CA.3 441]
MCKENZIE, RODERICK, Lieutenant of Highlanders, killed at Fort
DuQuesne 14.9 1758. [SM.XX.548]
MCKENZIE, W., Lieutenant of Highlanders, killed at Fort DuQuesne
14.9 1758. [SM.XX.548]
MCKENZIE, WILLIAM, in New York, piper and soldier of Captain Peter
Campbell of Glenure's Company, 1778. [SRO.GD170.3158]
MCKINNON, DONALD, soldier of the 84th Regiment 1783
[SRO GD174.2175]
MCKINNEN, ROBERT, of the 35th Regiment, who died in Pensacola,
West Florida. [Pro. 2.1767 PCC]
MCLACHLAN, DOUGALL, private of the 42nd Highlanders {Captain
Reid's Company} in New York 10 1757, killed in action.
[CA.3 441]
MACLAINE, Captain MURDOCH, 84th Regiment, in Charleston 1781-
1782. in New York 1783-1784. [SRO GD174.1338/2-3, 1286/7-8].
Lieutenant during French and Indian War prior to 1763. Captain of
84th{Royal Highland Emigrant} Regiment 1776-1783, land grants
near Halifax and Annapolis Royal, Nova Scotia, 1785
[SRO GD174.2177 6/7]
MCLAREN, DUNCAN, private in the 42nd Highlanders {Captain Reid's
Company} in New York 10 1757. [CA.3.441]
MCLAREN, JOHN, private of the 42nd Highlanders {Captain Reid's
Company} in New York 10.1757. [CA.3 441]
MACLEAN, ALEXANDER, born 1756, Lieutenant Colonel of the 2nd
West India Regiment and Commandant of the Bahama Islands, died
in Rothesay 1826. [Rothesay g/s]
MCLEAN, ALLAN, Lieutenant Colonel of the 84th [Royal Highland
Emigrant] Regiment 1775. [SRO.GD174.2091]
MCLEAN, ALLAN, born 23 4.1757, son of Reverend Hector MacLean
and Janet MacLean in Coll, an army officer, died at sea on voyage
home from New York. [F4.109]
MCLEAN, ARCHIBALD, Lieutenant of the New York Volunteers 1782.
[SRO GD174.2161]
MCLEAN, Captain ARCHIBALD, in New York 1784
[SRO.GD174.1361]
MCLEAN, DONALD, formerly of Montgomerie's Highlanders, an
overseer to James Penman in East Florida, 1769
[SRO.NRAS.771, bundle 491]
MCLEAN, FRANCIS, Captain of the 42nd Highlanders 1758, died in the
West Indies 1762. [OBW61]

MCLEAN, HECTOR, at Fort Edward 1779 |SRO.GD174.1321|

MACLEAN, JOHN, born 1724, son of Reverend Archibald MacLean and Susanna Campbell, tacksman of Scoune, Mull, admitted MFPSG in 1753, an army surgeon during the American Revolution. [F4.113]

MACLEAN, JOHN, born 15.4.1752, son of Reverend Alexander MacLean and Christian MacLean in Kilninian, Mull, Captain in the American Army, drowned near Halifax, Nova Scotia. [F4.115]

MCLEAN, JOHN, Lieutenant of the Royal Highland Emigrants 1778. [SRO GD174.1317]; [Cnf. 31.5.1783 Commisariat of Edinburgh]

MCLEAN, MALCOLM, soldier of the 2nd Battalion, 84th{Royal Highland Emigrant} Regiment in New York 15 7.1778. |SRO GD174.2120.3/4|

MACLEAN, MURDOCH, emigrated to America 1773, settled on the Kingsborough Patent, New York, Loyalist, Sergeant of the Royal Regiment of New York 1776-1783, settled in Charlottenburg, Ontario. |DFpp|

MACLEAN, Captain MURDOCH, of Colonel Myers West Indian Regiment.     |Cnf. 6 1.1797 Commisariat of Edinburgh|

MACLEAN, NEIL, Captain of the 21st {Royal Scots Fusiliers} Regiment, to America 1776, surrendered at Saratoga 17 10.1777. |RSF|

MACLEAN, NEIL, born 13.5 1736, son of Reverend Archibald MacLean and Susanna Campbell, Commisary at Niagara. [F.4.113]

MCLEAN, RODERICK, private of the 42nd Highlanders {Captain Reid's Company} in New York 10.1757. [CA.3.441]

MCLEISH, DONALD, private of the 42nd Highlanders {Captain Reid's Company} in New York 10.1757. [CA.3.441]

MCLEISH, DONALD, private of the 42nd Highlanders {Captain Reid's Company} in New York 10.1757. [CA.3.441]

MCLEOD, ALLAN, soldier of the 2nd Battalion, 84th {Royal Highland Emigrant} Regiment in New York 15 7.1778. [SRO.GD174.2120.3]

MCLEOD, MALCOLM, soldier in the French and Indians War, settled on the Kingsborough Patent, New York, by 1778, Loyalist, died 1778, wife and six children moved to Cornwall, Ontario [DFpp]

MCLEOD, NEIL, private of the 42nd Highlanders {Captain Reid's Company} in New York 10.1757. [CA.3.441]

MCLEOD, NORMAN, private of the 42nd Highlanders {Captain Reid's Company} in New York 10 1757, killed in action. [CA.3.441]

MACLEOD, NORMAN, Ensign of the 42nd Highlanders in New York 22.5 1757, Commissary at Niagara 1763, Captain of the 71st Regiment, wounded at Charleston 1780, surrendered at Yorktown. |NYSHA.X|

MCLEOD, NORMAN, Lieutenant of the 42nd Highlanders 1775, wounded at Fort Washington, killed at Yorktown 12.5 1781 [OBW63]

MCLEOD, NORMAND, soldier of the 2nd Battalion Royal Highlanders in Philadelphia 20.5.1778. [SRO GD174.2120.2]

MCLEOD, WILLIAM, emigrated to America 1773, settled on the Kingsborough Patent, New York, Loyalist, Lieutenant of the Royal Regiment of New York, settled in Charlottenburg, Ontario. [DFpp]

MCLEOD, ...., Captain of the 71st Regiment, wounded in South Carolina 1780 [SM.XXXXII.265]

MCLINNION, WILLIAM, private of the 42nd Highlanders {Captain Reid's Company} in New York 10.1757 [CA.3 441]

MCMILLAN, NEIL, private of the 42nd Highlanders {Captain Reid's Company} in New York 10.1757. [CA.3.441]

MCNAB, ARCHIBALD, Lieutenant of the 42nd Regiment, who died in New York. [Pro. 6 1767 PCC]

MCNAB, JAMES, Sergeant of the 42nd Highlanders {Captain John Reid's Company} in New York 10.1757 [CA.3 440]

MCNAUGHTON, ALEXANDER, Sergeant of the 2nd Battalion, 84th {Royal Highland Emigrant} Regiment, in New York 1778 [SRO GD174.2120.3/4]

MCNEAL, JOHN, grenadier, 42nd Highlanders, at Crown Point 3 9 1759 [NYSHA.X]

MCNEELAGE, DONALD, born in Argyll 1736, housecarpenter, deserted from the 1st Highland Regiment in America 1759 [New York Mercury, 4.6 1759]

MCNEIL, DONALD, private of the 42nd Highlandwers {Captain Reid's Company} in New York 10 1757 [CA.3.441]

MCNEIL, JOHN, Captain of the 42nd Highlanders, at New York 22.5.1757, Major 1762, died at Siege of Havanna 1762. [NYSHA.X][OBW63]

MCNEIL, NEIL, private of the 42nd Highlanders {Captain Reid's Company} in New York 10 1757. [CA.3 441]

MCNEILL, RODERICK, of Barra, Lieutenant of Fraser's Highlanders, killed on the Heights of Abraham, Quebec, 1760 [SHS.2.87]

MCNICOL, COLIN, soldier of the 77th Regiment, who died in Amboy, New Jersey. [Pro. 5 1764 PCC]

MCNICOLL, ......., soldier of the 84th {Royal Highland Emigrant} Regiment in New York 1778. [SRO GD174.2120 4]

MCPHEE, HUGH, private of the 42nd Highlanders {Captain Reid's Company} in New York 10.1757 [CA.3 441]

MCPHEE, JOHN, private of the 42nd Highlanders {Captain Reid's Company} in New York 10.1757. [CA.3.441]

MCPHERSON, ALEXANDER, private of the 42nd Highlanders {Captain Reid's Company} in New York 10.1757. [CA.3.441]

MCPHERSON, ALEXANDER, emigrated to America 1773, settled on the Kingsborough Patent, New York, Loyalist, soldier of the Royal Regiment of New York 1776-1783, settled in Edwardsburgh, Grenville County, Ontario. [DFpp]

MCPHERSON, COLIN, Quartermaster of the 42nd Regiment, who died in New York. [Pro.3 1765 PCC]

MCPHERSON, DONALD, private of the 42nd Highlanders {Captain Reid's Company} in New York 10.1757. [CA.3 441]

MCPHERSON, DUNCAN, Brevet Major of the 42nd Highlanders, wounded at York Island 17 9.1776, and at Pisquatua 10.5.1777. [OBW64]

MCPHERSON, HUGH, Lieutenant of the 42nd Highlanders in New York 22.5 1757, killed at Ticonderoga 7.1758. SM.XX.437][NYSHA.X][OBW64]

MCPHERSON, JAMES, a merchant in Edinburgh, then Lieutenant in Montgomery's Highlanders in America, 6.1759. [SRO CS16 105/78]

MCPHERSON, JOHN, Captain of the 17th Foot, a wounded prisoner after Battle of Princeton 1777. [SRO.NRAS.0771.247]

MCPHERSON, LAUCHLAN, emigrated to America, settled on the Kingsborough Patent, New York, by 1778, Loyalist, soldier of the Royal Regiment of New York. [DFpp]

MCPHERSON, MALCOLM, soldier in New England and Nova Scotia, 1758. [SRO.GD68.2/112]

MCPHERSON, MALCOLM, of Phones, born in Badenoch 1686, soldier at the Siege of Quebec 13.9.1759. [SM.XXI.662]

MCPHERSON, MURDOCH, emigrated to America on the Pearl 1773, soldier of the 22nd Regiment, settled on the Kingsborough Patent, New York, Loyalist, Sergeant of the Royal Regiment of New York, settled in Charlottenburg, Ontario. [DFpp]

MCQUEEN, DONALD, private of the 42nd Highlanders {Captain Reid's Company} in New York 10.1757, killed in action. [CA.3.441]

MCREA, WILLIAM, soldier of the 2nd Battalion, 84th {Royal Highland Emigrant} Regiment in New York 15.7.1778. [SRO GD174.2120.3]

MAITLAND, ALEXANDER, Colonel of the Foot Guards, allocated 12,000 acres in New York 1766. [PC Col.V.600]

MAITLAND, Hon. RICHARD, Lieutenant Colonel, Deputy Adjutant
General of HM Forces. [Pro. 7.1773 PCC]; married Mary McAdam
in New York 1772, allocated 12,000 acres in New York 1766.
[PC Col.V.600] [SRO.NRAS.0832.93]

MANT, THOMAS, Lieutenant of the 77th Regiment, allocated 10,000
acres in New York, and a 2,000 acre island between Lakes Erie and
St Clair, 18.6.1766. [PC Col.IV.818]

MARTIN, JOHN, Captain of the Royal North Carolina Regiment.
[Pro. 1.1793 PCC]

MELVILLE, ROBERT, Colonel of Foot in America, and as Brigadier
General in America, 1761. [SRO.GD126.box 29, 12/13]

MENZIES, ALEXANDER, Lieutenant of the 42nd Highlanders,
embarked for America 11 1757 [NYSHA.X][OBW66]

MENZIES, CHARLES, Ensign of the 42nd Highlanders {Captain John
Reid's Company} in New York 10.1757. [CA.3 440]

MENZIES, ROBERT, Major of the Fraser Highlanders, killed at Bushy
Run 1776.[SHS.2.112]

MERCER, COLIN, born 15.6.1731, son of Reverend James Mercer and
Elizabeth Logan in Aberdalgie, Perthshire, army surgeon, died in
Jamaica. [F4.194]

MERCER, JAMES, born 16 7 1725, son of Reverend James Mercer and
Elizabeth Logan in Aberdalgie, Perthshire, Captain of General
Webb's Regiment of Foot, who died at Fort Oswego, Albany, New
York, 13.8.1757. [Pro.2.1759 PCC] [F.4.194]

MERCER, JAMES FRANCIS, Perth, Lieutenant Colonel of Sir William
Pepperell's Regiment, who died at Oswego. [Pro. 7 1760 PCC]

MILL, THOMAS, soldier of the 55th Regiment, discharged in Halifax,
Nova Scotia, 1765, a Loyalist in New York, settled in Halifax,
Nova Scotia, 1784. [PRO.AO13 14.358/362]

MILLER, DAVID, Lieutenant of the 42nd Highlanders, wounded at
Ticonderoga 7.1758. [OBW67][SM.XX.437]

MILLIGAN, WILLIAM, mason, 42nd Highlanders, at Crown Point
17.8.1759. [NYSHA.X]

MILLS, DAVID, Lieutenant of the 42nd Highlanders, in North America
1759 [OBW67]

MILNE, DAVID, Lieutenant of the 42nd Highlanders, embarked for
America 11.1757, wounded at Ticonderoga 1758, wounded in
Martinique 1762. [NYSHA.X]

MILNE, JAMES, Lieutenant and surgeon of the 2nd Battalion of Royal
Americans, surgeon of the hospital at Fort Pitt. [Pro. 1.1765 PCC]

MITCHELL, JAMES, private of the 42nd Highlanders {Captain Reid's
Company} in New York 10 1757 [CA.3 441]

MONCRIEF, WILLIAM, Captain of the Queen's Rangers, who died at New York, son of James Moncrief. [Pro. 2.1790 PCC]

MONTGOMERY, ARCHIBALD, Colonel of the 77th Foot, 1758-1759. [SRO GD21.2/87/1-4]

MUNRO, HUGH, former NCO of the 77th Regiment, received a land grant of a 48 acre island in the Hudson River, near Albany, opposite Fort Edward, 5.8.1766. [NY Col. MS.7 903]

MUNROE, HUGH, emigrated to America 1774, settled on the Kingsborough Patent, New York, Loyalist, soldier of the Royal Regiment of New York 1776-1783, settled at River aux Raisons, Ontario. [DFpp]

MUNRO, MALCOLM, Sergeant in Captain John McNeill's Company of the 1st Battalion, the Highland Regiment, who died in Long Island, New York. [Pro.5.1766 PCC]

MUNRO, Captain of Highlanders, killed at Fort DuQuesne 14.9 1758. [SM.XX.548]

MURCHISON, DUNCAN, emigrated to America 1773, settled on the Kingsborough Patent, New York, Loyalist, soldier of the Royal Regiment of New York, settled in Canada. [DFpp]

MURCHISON, JOHN, emigrated to America 1773, settled on the Kingsborough Patent, New York, Loyalist, soldier of the Royal Regiment of New York, settled in Charlottenburg, Ontario, 1783. [DFpp]

MURDOFF, GEORGE, emigrated to America 1773, settled on the Kingsborough Patent, New York, Loyalist, soldier in the Royal Regiment of New York, settled in Fredericksburgh, Ontario. [DFpp]

MURRAY, DONALD, private of the 42nd Highlanders {Captain Reid's Company} in New York 10.1757. [CA.3.441]

MURRAY, JAMES, private of the 42nd Regiment {Captain Reid's Company} in New York 10.1757. [CA.3.441]

MURRAY, JAMES, born 19..3.1734 at Tullibardine, son of Lord George Murray and Amelia Murray, Captain of the 42nd Highlanders, embarked for America 11.1757, wounded at Ticonderoga 7 1758, and wounded at Martinique, returned to America 3.1777, at battles of Brandywine and Germantown 1777. Died in London 19.3.1794 [NYSHA.X][SM.XX.437]

MURRAY, JAMES, Lieutenant of Fraser's Highlanders, killed at Louisbourg 6.1758. [SHS.2.87]

MURRAY, JAMES, former Captain of the Queen's American Rangers, died in Norfolk, Virginia, 29.3.1789 [SM.51.361]

MURRAY, JOHN, Edinburgh, Captain Lieutenant of the 55th Foot in
North America. [Pro. 5.1759 PCC]

MURRAY, WILLIAM, Lieutenant Colonel of the 27th Regiment in
America 1777. [SRO.GD68.2/117]

MURRAY, Captain, 48th Regiment in New York 1777
[SRO.NRAS.0696.2]

MURRAY, Sergeant, 42nd Highlanders, at Ticonderoga 24 7 1759.
[NYSHA.X]

OGILVIE, WILLIAM, Captain of an Independent Company in New York.
[Pro. 8.1763 PCC]

PEEBLES, JOHN, first surgeon's mate of the 2nd Virginia
Regiment,1758. [SRO GD21.674] wounded at Bushy Run
6.8.1763; Captain of the 42nd Regiment 1772-1782, from Greenock
to Boston, and from Boston to Halifax 1776, in New York 1776-
1779, wounded in Charleston 1779-1780, returned to New York
1780-1782, returned to Scotland, died 1824.
[SRO GD21.492][OBW72][SM.XXV.575]

PETRIE, GEORGE, Captain of the 21st {Royal Scots Fusiliers}
Regiment, to America 1776, surrendered at Saratoga 17 10 1777
[RSF]

PITCAIRN, JOHN, born 1722, Major in the Royal Marines, died at
Bunker Hill, Boston, 19.4.1775. [F.5.87]

RATTRAY, GEORGE, son of Rattray of Dalrunzion, Ensign of the 42nd
Regiment, embarked for America 11 1757, killed at Ticonderoga
7 1758.[OBW74] [NYSHA.X][SM.XX.437]

REA, JAMES, private of the 42nd Highlanders {Captain Reid's
Company} in New York 10 1757. [CA.3 441]

REID, ALEXANDER, private of the 42nd Highlanders {Captain Reid's
Company} in New York 10.1757. [CA.3.441]

REID, JAMES, disbanded soldier, allocated 250 acres in Albany County,
New York, 15.8.1766 [N.Y Col. MS.7.903]

REID, JOHN, of Straloch, Captain of the 42nd Highlanders, at New York
22.5 1757, wounded at Martinique, died 1808.
[NYSHA.X][OBW74]

ROBERTSON, DONALD, private of the 42nd Highlanders {Captain
Reid's Company} in New York 10. 1757 [CA.3 441]

ROBERTSON, JAMES, General, in America 1756-1783, Barrackmaster
General in America 1765-1776, Governor of New York 1779-1783
[SRO.GD172]

ROBINSON, JOHN, carpenter, 42nd Highlanders, at Ticonderoga
25 7.1759. [NYSHA.X]

ROLLO, CHARLES, Lieutenant Colonel of the 22nd Foot at Schenectady 11 1757.[SRO.GD45: 2/19/1-4]

ROSS, ALEXANDER, private of the 42nd Highlanders {Captain Reid's Company} in New York 10.1757. [CA.3.441]

ROSS, DONALD, private of the 42nd Highlanders {Captain Reid's Company} in New York 10 1757. [CA.3.441]

ROSS, DONALD, emigrated to America, soldier during the French and Indian Wars, settled on the Kingsborough Patent, New York, 1763, Loyalist, soldier of the Royal Regiment of New York 1776-1777, died 1787. [DFpp]

ROSS, FINLAY, born 1740, emigrated to America, settled on the Kingsborough Patent, New York, Loyalist, soldier of the Royal Regiment of New York, settled in Charlottenburg, Ontario, died 1830 [DFpp]

ROSS, HUGH, private in the 42nd Highlanders {Captain Reid's Company} in New York 10.1757, killed in action. [CA.3.441]

ROSS, JOHN, private of the 42nd Highlanders {Captain Reid's Company} in New York 10 1757 [CA.3.441]

ROSS, JOHN, Lieutenant of 71st Regiment of Grenadiers, prisoner of the Americans, late 1781 in New York. [SRO.15.44/103]

ROSS, JOHN Captain of the 31st Regiment, allocated 5,000 acres of land in West Florida 5.1765. [PC Col.IV.814]

ROSS, THOMAS, tailor, emigrated to America 1772, settled on the Kingsborough Patent, New York, by 9.1773, Loyalist, soldier in the Royal Regiment of New York, settled in Lancaster, Glengarry County, Ontario. [DFpp]

ROSS, THOMAS, born in Drumvaich, emigrated to America 1773, settled on the Kingsborough Patent, New York, Loyalist, soldier in the Royal Regiment of New York 1776-1783, settled in Cornwall, Ontario. [DFpp]

ROSS, THOMAS BANE, born in Creich, Sutherland, 1729, soldier at Quebec 1763, settled on the Kingsborough Patent, New York before 1778, Loyalist, soldier in the Royal Regiment of New York 1779-1783, settled in Lancaster, Ontario, buried in South Lancaster Cemetery 10.8.1806. [DFpp]

ROSS, THOMAS, of Culrossie, Captain of Fraser's Highlanders, killed on the Heights of Abraham, 1759.[SHS.2. 87]

RUTHERFORD, WALTER, Major of the 1st {Royal Scots} Regiment, allocated 5,000 acres in New York 2.1765. [PC Col.IV.818]

ST CLAIR, ARTHUR, soldier in North America 1757-1758. [SRO GD69.171]

SHAW, LACHLAN, Lieutenant of Captain Paul Demeri's Independent Company in South Carolina. [Pro. 2.1765 PCC]; [Cnf. 1.12.1762 Commissariat of Edinburgh]

SHAW, NEIL, private of the 42nd Highlanders {Captain Reid's Company} in New York 10 1757 [CA.3.441]

SINCLAIR, ALEXANDER, born 1748, a labourer, deserted from the 1st Battalion, the Royal American Regiment, in 1772. [New York Gazette & Weekly Mercury, 12.10 1772]

SINCLAIR, CHARLES, Ensign of the 78th {Fraser Highlanders} Regiment, land grant in Albany County, New York, 1773 [PC Col.V.598]

SINCLAIR, JOHN, private of the 42nd Highlanders {Captain Reid's Company} in New York 10 1757, died of wounds. [CA.3 441]

SINCLAIR, Corporal, 42nd Highlanders, at Crown Point, 7.8.1759 [NYSHA.X]

SMALL, JOHN, born in Strathardle, Perthshire, son of Patrick Small and Magdalen Robertson, to America 1756, Lieutenant of the 42nd Highlanders in New York 22.4.1757, at Ticonderoga, Lake Champlain, and Montreal, and in 1762 in Havanna and Martinique, later a Brigadier General at Bunker Hill 1776, Lieutenant Commander of the 2nd Battalion 84th Royal Highland Emigrants, at Fort Edward, New York, 1783, died in Guernsey [NYSHA.X][OBW80]

SMALL, JOHN, Major of the Royal Highland Emigrant Regiment in Charleston 1775, in Halifax 1778. [SRO GD174.2092; 2116]

SMITH, DANIEL, son of Mrs Hannah Smith, soldier of Captain McNeil's Company, the 42nd Regiment of Foot, who died in Elizabethtown, near New York. [Pro. 4.1766 PCC]

SMITH, JOHN, private of the 42nd Highlanders {Captain Reid's Company} in New York 10.1757. [CA.3 441]

SMITH, JOHN, Ensign of the 42nd Highlanders, wounded at Ticonderoga 7.1758. [SM.XX.437]

SPALDING, WALTER, private of the 42nd Highlanders {Captain Reid's Company} in New York 10 1757 [CA.3 441]

SPOTSWOOD, ALEXANDER, Orange County, Virginia, died in Annapolis, Maryland, late Major General and Colonel of the American Regiment. [Pro. 2.1742 PCC]

STEWART, ALEXANDER, Lieutenant of General James Oglethorpe's Regiment, who died in Fredericia, Georgia. [Pro. 4.1748 PCC]

STEWART, ALEXANDER, private of the 42nd Highlanders {Captain Reid's Company} in New York 10 1757. [CA.3 441]

STEWART, ALEXANDER, Sergeant in Captain Stirling's Company of
1st Battalion, 42nd Regiment, who died in New York.
[Pro 1.1766 PCC]

STEWART, CHARLES, private of the 42nd Highlanders {Captain Reid's
Company} in New York 10.1757, died of wounds. [CA.3.441]

STEWART, DONALD, private of the 42nd Highlanders {Captain Reid's
Company} in New York 10.1757, died of wounds [CA.3.441]

STEWART, DUNCAN, son of Stewart of Derculich, Ensign of the 42nd
Regiment, embarked for America 11.1757. [NYSHA.X]

STEWART, JAMES younger of Urrard, Captain of the 42nd Highlanders,
embarked for America 11.1757, wounded at Ticeronderoga 7 1758.
[NYSHA X][OBW82][SM XX.437]

STEWART, JOHN, volunteer in the 2nd Battalion Royal Highland
Emigrants in New York 15.7.1778. [SRO.GD174.2120.3]

STEWART, JOHN, Corporal of the 42nd Highlanders {Captain John
Reid's Company} in New York 10.1757. [CA.3.440]

STEWART, JOHN, mason, 42nd Highlanders, at Crown Point 16.8.1759.
[NYSHA X]

STEWART, PATRICK, son of Stewart of Bonskied, Ensign of the 42nd
Regiment in New York 22.5 1757, killed at Ticonderoga 7.1758.
[NYSHA X][OBW83][SM XX 437]

STEWART, WALTER, private of the 42nd Highlanders {Captain Reid's
Company} in New York 10.1757, died of wounds. [CA.3.441]

STEWART, WILLIAM, son of William Stewart of Garth, Lieutenant of
the 42nd Highlanders, wounded at Pisquatua 1777. [OBW83]

STIRLING, GEORGE, Edinburgh, son of John Stirling in Glasgow,
Lieutenant of General Oglethorpe's Regiment, who died in Georgia.
[Pro 1.1749 PCC]

STIRLING, THOMAS, younger of Ardoch, born 8 10 1731,second son of
Sir Henry Stirling of Ardoch, Captain of the 42nd Highlanders,
embarked for America 11.1757, wounded in Martinique, to
Havanna and Martinique 1762, to Fort de Chartres on the
Mississippi 8.1765, returned to Scotland, to America as Lieutenant
Colonel of the 42nd Highlanders1776, fought at Brooklyn, Fort
Washington, Monmouth, etc, died 9.5.1808 .
[NYSHA.X][SRO.GD24.1.458][SRO.RI14.22][OBW84]

STUART, FRANCIS, Captain of the 26th Regiment, died in New York,
husband of Mary Stuart. [Pro. 5.1779 PCC]

STUART, Hon. JAMES, Lieutenant Colonel of the 1st Regiment of
Guards, who died at Guildford, America, son of Lady Margaret
Blantyre. [Pro. 8.1781 PCC]

SUTHERLAND, ALEXANDER, soldier, 42nd Highlanders, at Crown
Point 27.8.1759 [NYSHA.X]
SUTHERLAND, JOHN, Lieutenant of the 42nd Highlanders in New York
22.4 1757, killed at Ticonderoga 7 1758.
[NYSHA.X][OBW85][SM.XX.437]
SUTHERLAND, Captain WILLIAM, ADC to Sir H. Clinton in New
York 1778. [SRO GD153.box 1]
TAYLOR, JOSEPH, soldier of the 2nd Battalion, 84th [Royal Highland
Emigrant] Regiment in New York 15.7.1778.
[SRO GD174.2120.3]
TAYLOR, SAMUEL, soldier of the 2nd Battalion, 84th [Royal Highland
Emigrant] Regiment in New York 15 7.1778.
[SRO GD174.2120.3]
TOLMIE, KENNETH, Lieutenant of the 42nd Highlanders [Captain John
Reid's Company] at New York 22.5.1757, at Crown Point
25.9 1759. [CA.3.440][NYSHA.X][OBW86]
TRAILL, GEORGE, assistant surgeon in a military hospital in North
America, son of John Traill in Edinburgh. [Pro. 10 1759 PCC]
TURNBULL, ALEXANDER, of Stracathro, Lieutenant of the 42nd
Highlanders in New York 22.5.1757, wounded in Martinique, died
1804 [NYSHA.X][OBW86]
TURNBULL, Lieutenant Colonel GEORGE, "served in the British Army
for over 60 years", died in New York 13 10 1810
[Edinburgh Advertiser, 4908.373]
TURNER, ARCHIBALD, born 1761, soldier of the 2nd Battalion, Royal
Highland Regiment, in Philadelphia 20.5.1778
[SRO GD174.2120.2]
URQUHART, ROBERT, private of the 42nd Highlanders [Captain Reid's
Company] in New York 10.1757. [CA.3.441]
URQUHART, WILLIAM, emigrated to America 1773, settled on the
Kingsborough Patent, New York, Loyalist, soldier of the Royal
Regiment of New York 1776-1783, settled at River aux Raison,
Charlottenburg, Ontario. [DFpp]
WATSON, DONALD, private of the 42nd Highlanders [Captain Reid's
Company] in New York 10.1757 [CA.3 441]
WATSON, JOHN, Sergeant of the 42nd Highlanders [Captain John
Reid's Company] in New York 10 1757 [CA.3 440]
WATSON, JOHN, born in Dalranick, Inverness, 1738, labourer, deserted
from the 55th Regiment of Foot in America 1759
[New York Mercury, 12.3.1759]
WEBSTER, ....., son of Reverend Dr Webster, killed in action 1781
[SRO GD69.300]

WELSH, THOMAS, soldier of the 2nd Battalion 84th {Royal Highland Emigrant} Regiment in Philadelphia 20.5.1778, in New York 15 7 1778. [SRO.GD174.2120.3]

WHEET, DONALD, private of the 42nd Highlanders {Captain Reid's Company} in New York 10.1757. [CA.3 441]

WHITE, WILLIAM, soldier of the 84th {Royal Highland Emigrant} Regiment in New York 15.7.1778. [SRO.GD174.2120.3/4]

WHITLEY, ROGER, possibly from Edinburgh, of General Nicholson's Independent Company, died at Fort King George, South Carolina. [Pro. 12.1729 PCC]

WILKIESON, DONALD, soldier of the 2nd Battalion,84th {Royal Highland Emigrant} Regiment in New York 15.7.1778. [SRO GD2120.3/4]

WILSON,....., Lieutenant of the 71st Regiment, wounded in South Carolina 1780. [SM.XXXXII.265]

WISHART, WILLIAM, private of the 42nd Highlanders {Captain Reid's Company} in New York 10 1757. [CA.3.441]

WRIGHT, DUNCAN, private of the 42nd Highlanders {Captain Reid's Company} in New York 10.1757. [CA.3.441]

YOUNG, JOHN, Colonel of the Royal American Regiment, husband of Anne Pringle, 1761 [SRO.RS27 157.341]; [Cnf 31.5.1766 Commissariat of Edinburgh]

YOUNG, THEOPHILIUS, Lieutenant of the 45th Regiment, died at Louisbourg, son of Thomas Young. [Pro.11.1787 PCC]

# *SCOTTISH SOLDIER,*

# *IN*

# *COLONIAL AMERICA*

## Part Two

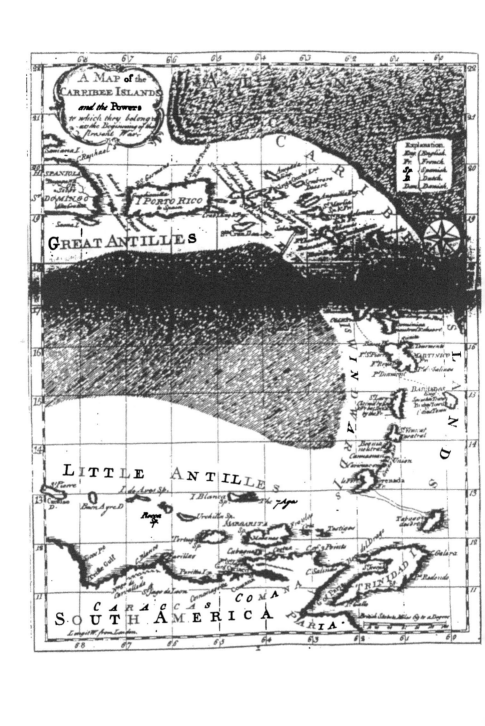

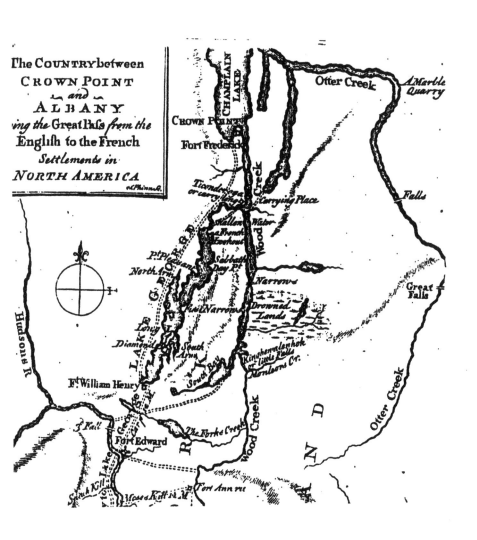

The COUNTRY between
CROWN POINT
and
ALBANY
...ing the Great Pass from the
English to the French
Settlements in
NORTH AMERICA
M.Phinn.R.

Otter Creek

A Marble
Quarry

CHAMPLAIN LAKE

CROWN POINT

Fort Frederick

Wood Creek

Falls

Ticonderoga
or carrying place

Carrying Place

Wallens Water

a French
Sawhouse

Pt.Pleasant

Sabbath
Day Pt

North Arm

Narrows

Great
Falls

LAKE GEORGE

The Narrows

Drowned
Lands

Long I.

Diamond I.

South
Arm

South Bay

Kinghemalanhok
or little Falls
Monloons Cr.

Ft. William Henry

Hudsons R.

3.d Fall

LAKE GEORGE RIVER

Fort Edward

The Forks Creek

Wood Creek

Otter Creek

N D

Spruk Kill

Mosea Kill I.M

Fort Ann ru

# INTRODUCTION

From as early as the 1650s there were Scots serving in the colonial militia forces of New England and possibly of Virginia. These men had arrived in America in chains as prisoners of war captured after Worcester and other battles of the Civil War and subsequently transported to the colonies as indentured servants. However it was not until the mid eighteenth century that the British Government began to despatch Highland Regiments, such as Fraser's Highlanders, the Black Watch, and Montgomery's Highlanders to America. The Seven Years War 1756-1763, otherwise kn+own as the French and Indian War, led to significant recruitment in Scotland, particularly in the Highlands, for service in the American colonies. The experience gained by these soldiers was to influence their decision to subsequently settle or emigrate to America. The allocation of land to former military personnel in the aftermath of the war was a major incentive. The massive increase in emigration to America from the Highlands that occurred in the decade after the Seven Years War resulted to some extent from the influence of returning soldiers. On the outbreak of the American War of Independence, alias the American Revolution, former soldiers who had received land grants were recalled for duty by the British Government. For example many former Scottish soldiers who had been settled in the Mohawk Valley in upper New York were recruited into the King's Royal Regiment of New York. At the same time many new or recent immigrants from Scotland formed the Royal Highland Emigrant Regiment. After the war large numbers of soldiers from Loyalist units and from regular British Army regiments, including many Scots, were settled in what have become Nova Scotia, Prince Edward Island, New Brunswick, Ontario and Quebec. Scottish soldiers thus not only played an important role in defending the American colonies but also a prominent role in settling them. This book, the second of a series, attempts to identify individual soldiers and is based on research into both manuscript and printed material.

David Dobson
St Andrews, 1997

# SCOTTISH SOLDIERS
# IN COLONIAL AMERICA

## [Part Two]

ABERCROMBY, Sir JAMES, born at Glassbaugh 1706, to America in
　　1756 as a Major General, Commander in Chief there 1758, at
　　Fort Ticonderoga 8.7.1758, died 28.4.1781. [ANY.1.27]
ABERNATHY, WILLIAM, soldier of the Black Watch, land grant by the
　　Nashwaak River, New Brunswick, 1785. [PANB:MC315]
ADAM, JOHN, born in Scotland 1729, settled in Caroline County,
　　Virginia, militiaman of the Virginia Regiment 1757. [VMHB.1][L]
AFFLECK, PHILIP, Lieutenant in the Royal Navy, given a land grant in
　　New York 1773. [ActsPCCol.V.597]
AGNEW, ANDREW, Lieutenant of the 93rd Highlanders in Nova Scotia
　　and in Canada, ca.1838-1841. [SRO.GD154.745.1/16]
ANDERSON, ALEXANDER, born in Scotland 1735, settled in Augusta
　　County, Virginia, militiaman of the Virginia Regiment 1757.
　　[VMHB.1][L]
AUSTIN, WILLIAM, surgeon's mate at HM Hospital in North America,
　　who died at Albany, New York, son of Joseph Austin in Kilspindie,
　　Perthshire, pro 12.1764 PCC
BAIN, ALEXANDER, soldier of the Black Watch, land grant by the
　　Nashwaak River, New Brunswick, 1785. [PANB:MC315]
BALLENTINE, DAVID, born in Strathaven 1760, soldier of the 82nd
　　Regiment, land grant of 2,000 acres on Cape Louis {Cape George},
　　Nova Scotia, 1783, died there 1843. [HA10]
BARCLAY, DAVID, a former Captain and Paymaster of the 76th
　　{McDonald's Highlanders} Regiment, a prisoner at Yorktown, died
　　in Southampton 1807. [AJ#3125]
BARRACK, JOHN, born in Scotland 1716, a tailor at Fort Cumberland,
　　Maryland, and a militiaman of the Virginia Regiment 1756. [L]
BENNET, CHARLES, born 1727 in Aberdeenshire, Ensign of Fraser's
　　Highlanders in America. [AJ#3125]

1

BISSETT, JOHN, born in Scotland 1733, a schoolmaster in Stafford County, Virginia, and a militiaman of the Virginia Regiment 1756.[VMHB.1/2][L]

BLAIR, GEORGE, soldier of the Black Watch, land grant by the Nashwaak River, New Brunswick, 1785. [PANB: MC315]

BROWN, Colonel JAMES, in Barbados, 1664. [RGS.XI.553]

BROWN, JOHN, born 1773, son of Samuel Brown and Mary Thomson, a surgeon in the 42nd Regiment, died in St Vincent 9.1796. [Senwick g/s]

BRUCE, DAVID, soldier of the Black Watch, wife, land grant by the Nashwaak River, New Brunswick, 1785. [PANB: MC315]

BRUCE, JOHN, soldier of the Black Watch, land grant by the Nashwaak River, New Brunswick, 1785. [PANB: MC315]

BUCHAN, WILLIAM, soldier of the Black Watch, wife, land grant by the Nashwaak River, New Brunswick, 1785. [PANB:MC315]

BUCHANAN, JAMES, born in Scotland 1736, a militiaman of the Virginia Regiment 1756. [VMHB.1/2][L]

BURGESS, JOHN, master gunner and bombardier at Annapolis Royal, 1714. [Laing Charters,#3074]

CAMERON, ANGUS, emigrated to America 1773, settled on the Kingsborough Patent, New York, Loyalist, soldier of the Royal Regiment of New York, settled in Charlottenburgh, Ontario. [DFpp]

CAMERON, DONALD, Urquhart, Inverness-shire, soldier of the 84th [Royal Highland Emigrants] Regiment, land grant at Upper Settlement, East River, Pictou, Nova Scotia, 1784. [SG.III.3.98]

CAMERON, JAMES, soldier of the Black Watch, land grant by the Nashwaak River, New Brunswick, 1785. [PANB: MC315]

CAMERON, JOHN, soldier of the Black Watch, land grant on the Nashwaak River, New Brunswick, 1785. [PANB: MC315]

CAMERON, JOHN, soldier of the 54th Regiment, land grant by the Nashwaak River, New Brunswick, 1785. [PANB: MC315]

CAMERON, JOHN, emigrated to America 1773, settled on the Kingsborough Patent, New York, Loyalist, soldier of the 1st Battalion of the Royal Regiment of New York, dead by 1788. [DFpp]

CAMERON, JOHN MCAFEE, emigrated from Fort William to America on the Pearl 1773, settled on the Kingsborough Patent, New York, Loyalist, soldier of the Royal Regiment of New York 1776-1783, settled in Fairfield, Lancaster, Glengarry County, Ontario, 1784. [DFpp]

CAMERON, WILLIAM BUY, emigrated to America 1774, settled on the Kingsborough Patent, New York, soldier of the Royal Regiment of New York, settled in Charlottenburgh, Ontario. [DFpp]

CAMPBELL, ALEXANDER, Captain of the 62nd Foot, a Major in Portuguese Service, died in Tobago 7.1767. [AJ#1029]

CAMPBELL, ALEXANDER, Major of the 77th{Montgomery's Highlanders} 1757, with General Forbes on the expedition to Fort Pitt 1758, with Amherst to Lake Champlain 1759, member of the St Andrew's Society of New York 1761, Lieutenant General 1801, died 1804. [ANY.1.40][SRO.GD37.1.73/74]

CAMPBELL, ALEXANDER, Lieutenant Colonel of the 78th Regiment, given a land grant in New York 1773. [ActsPCCol.V.598]

CAMPBELL, ALLAN, son of Barcaldine, Ensign of the 42nd Regiment 1745, to America in 1756 as Captain of the 42nd Highlanders at Ticonderoga, a Major under Amherst in 1759, member of the St Andrew's Society of New York 1762, allocated 5000 acres at Crown Point 1763, Major of the 36th Foot in Jamaica 1770, Major General 1780, died 1795. [ANY.1.47][SRO.GD87.1.82]

CAMPBELL, ANGUS, Captain of the 37th Regiment, son of Campbell of Forrighty, died in St Vincent 1801. [AJ#2794]

CAMPBELL, ARCHIBALD, of Glen Lyon, Lieutenant of 78th (Fraser's Highlanders) Regiment 1757, in New York 1757, Captain 1760.[ANY.1.17]

CAMPBELL, DONALD, Lieutenant of the 77th Foot, wounded at Bushy Run 6.8.1763. [AJ#822]

CAMPBELL, DONALD, born 23.7.1730, son of Lachlan and Martha Campbell in Lorine, Islay, settled in New York, an army officer, died in Washington, DC, 1803. [ANY.1.5]

CAMPBELL, DOUGAL, born in Scotland 1726, a carpenter at Fort Cumberland, Maryland, and a militiaman of the Virginia Regiment 1756. [VMHB.1/2][L]

CAMPBELL, Major DOUGAL, Chief Engineer in North America, died on passage from Halifax to New York 10.1757. [SM.19.614]

CAMPBELL, DUGALD, Lieutenant of the Black Watch, wife and 2 children, land grant by the Nashwaak River, New Brunswick, 1785. [PANB:MC315]

CAMPBELL, DUGALD, soldier of the Black Watch, land grant by the Nashwaak River, New Brunswick, 1785. [PANB: MC315]

CAMPBELL, D., born 1782, Captain of the 91st Argyll Regiment, died 29.11.1824.[Spanish Town Cathedral, Jamaica, g/s]

CAMPBELL, DUNCAN, Lieutenant of the 42nd Foot, wounded at Bushy Run 6.8.1763. [AJ#822]

CAMPBELL, HUGH, born in Scotland 1731, settled in King William County, Virginia, a militiaman of the Virginia Regiment 1756. [VMHB.1/2][L]

CAMPBELL, JAMES, born in Scotland 1738, settled in Stafford County, Virginia, a militiaman of the Virginia Regiment 1757. [VMHB.1/2][L]

CAMPBELL, JOHN, born in Scotland 1726, a planter in Alexandria, Virginia, and a militiaman of the Virginia Regiment 1756. [VMHB.1/2][L]

CAMPBELL, JOHN, of Glen Daruel, born 1731, Officer of the 42nd Royal Highlanders 1745-, wounded at Ticonderoga 1758, fought in Canada, Martinique and Havana, member of the St Andrew's Society of New York 1760, died in Montreal 23.6.1795. [ANY.1.36]

CAMPBELL, JOHN, of Strachur, Lieutenant of Loudoun's Highlanders 6.1745, officer of the 42nd Highlanders wounded at Ticonderoga 1758, Major in 1759, member of the St Andrew's Society of New York 1761, Lieutenant Colonel 1762, fought in Martinique and in Havana, to America as Colonel of the 57th Foot 1776, Commander of British Forces in West Florida, surrendered Pensacola to the Spanish 10.5.1781, General 1797, died 28.8.1806. [ANY.1.41]

CAMPBELL, JOHN, Lieutenant, land grant in West Florida 11.2.1771. [Acts.PCCol.V.594]

CAMPBELL, JOHN, Lieutenant Colonel of the 78th Regiment, given a land grant in New York 1773. [ActsPCCol.V.598]

CAMPBELL, MUNGO, Captain of the 77th Montgomery's Highlanders 15.9.1758, Captain 1760, Major 1770, commander of Fort Brewerton at the outlet of Oneida Lake, member of the St Andrew's Society of New York 1762, killed leading the attack on Fort St Anne at the Battle of White Plains 1777. [ANY.1.47]

CARMICHAEL, JAMES, born in Scotland 1737, a joiner in Prince George County, Virginia, and a militiaman of the Virginia Regiment 1757. [VMHB.1/2][L]

CARR, THOMAS, born in Scotland 1716, a piper and a militiaman of the Virginia Regiment 1756. [VNHB.1/2][L]

CHISHOLM, JAMES, emigrated from Loch Broom to America 1775, arrived in Philadelphia 6.10.1775, Revolutionary Army Officer, in New York 1789. [SRO.NRAS.771, bundle 700]

CLELAND, DANIEL, of the Canadian Rifles, son of James Cleland and Janet Douglas in Whitburn, 1856. [SRO.S/H.1856]

CLEPHANE, JAMES, Officer of the Scots Brigade in Dutch Service by 1747, Officer of the 78th {Fraser's Highlanders} Regiment 1757, fought at the Siege of Louisbourg. [ANY.1.30]

COCHRANE, HUGH, born in Scotland or Ulster, deserted from the Newport, Rhode Island, Regiment 1760. [New York Mercury, 5.5.1760]

COCHRANE, JAMES, Lieutenant Colonel of Oglethorpe's Regiment in Georgia 1730s. [PRO.CO5.670.334]

COCKBURN, DOUGLAS, Lieutenant of the South Carolina Regiment of Royalists, Edinburgh, cnf 14.10.1793 Edinburgh

COCKBURN, JAMES, Ensign in Lord John Murray's Regiment of Foot in North America 1746. [SRO.GD216.188]

COLE, JOHN, born in Scotland 1736, a planter in Prince William County, Virginia, and a militiaman of the Virginia Regiment 1756. [VMHB.1/2][L]

COLTBERT, WILLIAM, born in Scotland 1734, a smith and planter in Westmoreland County, Virginia, a militiaman of the Virginia Regiment 1756. [VMHB.1/2][L]

CORBETT, DAVID, Captain of the 47th Regiment of Foot, died at Fort Charlotte, Nassau, New Providence, 1801. [AJ#2778]

CRAM, PETER, born in Scotland 1732, a planter in Stafford County, Virginia, and a militiaman of the Virginia Regiment 1756. [VMHB.1/2][L]

CRAWFORD, JOHN WALKINGSHAW, of Craufordland, born 1721, British Army officer 1741-, Captain of the 78th (Fraser's Highlanders) Regiment during French and Indian War, at Quebec 1759, died 1793. [ANY.1.19]

CROOKBANE, JOHN, born in Scotland 1736, a silversmith in Fredericksburg, Virginia, and a militiaman of the Virginia Regiment 1756. [VMHB.1/2][L]

CURRY, WILLIAM, a Scot who deserted from the British Army in Petersburg, Virginia, 1754. [Va.Gaz.19.7.1754]

CUTHBERT, JOHN, of Drackies, Inverness-shire, to Georgia 1735, Ranger Captain there 1738.[PRO.CO5.670.21/9][GA.Council Rec.10.5.1738]

DALRYMPLE, Colonel CAMPBELL, former Governor of Guadaloupe, 1764. [SRO.RS.27{Edinburgh}166.335]

DANIELS, WILLIAM, soldier of the Black Watch, land grant by the Nashwaak River, New Brunswick, 1785. [PANB:MC315]

DEWAR, JOHN, born Perth 1745, emigrated to New York 1768, soldier
of the King's Royal Regiment of New York, settled in Caldwell
Manor, Quebec, 1783, Captain of Militia in 1812. [Missisquoi
County Historical Society]

DOW, JAMES, Lieutenant of the 60th Regiment, wounded at Bushy Run
6.8.1763. [AJ#822]

DRUMMOND, ALEXANDER, Surgeon, late of the King's American
Regiment, land grant by the Nashwaak River, New Brunswick,
1785. [PANB: MC315]

DUNCAN, WILLIAM, Sergeant of the 4th Regiment of Foot, died in
Guadaloupe, cnf 27.5.1762 Edinburgh

DUNDAS, RALPH, prisoner of the French after the Battle of Yorktown
1781. [SRO.GD35.57.13]

DUNDAS, Major General THOMAS, born 1750, died at Fort Matilda,
Guadaloupe. [Trinidad monumental inscription]

ERSKINE, ROBERT, born 7.9.1735 in Dunfermline son of Reverend
Ralph Erskine and Margaret Simson, Geographer and Surveyor
General of the US Army, died 2.10.1780. [F.5.30]

EVANS, EDWARD, born in Scotland 1734, settled in Fredericksburg,
Virginia, a drummer in the Virginia Regiment 1757.
[VMHB.1/2][L]

FARQUHAR, ALEXANDER, on the Expedition to Fort Levi, Isle
Royale, 1760. [SRO.RH1.2.776]

FARQUHAR, PATRICK GELLIE, Captain of the 66th Regiment of Foot
commanded by Lord Adam Gordon, died in Jamaica 1764.
[AJ#881]

FARQUHARSON, ALEXANDER, Lieutenant of the 42nd Highlanders in
Montreal 1760. [SRO.RH1.2.765]

FEGAN, JOHN, born in Scotland 1730, soldier of the Virginia Militia
1756. [VMHB.1/2][L]

FERGUSON, ALEXANDER, emigrated to America 1773, settled on the
Kingsborough Patent, New York, Loyalist, soldier of the Royal
Regiment of New York 1776-1783, dead by 1788. [DFpp]

FERGUSON, ANDREW, Captain of the Royal Artillery, died in Halifax,
Nova Scotia, 1766. [AJ#952]

FERGUSON, DUNCAN, born in Scotland 1732, settled in Winchester
County, Virginia, a drummer of the Virginia Regiment 1756.
[VMHB.1/2][L]

FERGUSON, PETER, emigrated to America 1773, settled on the
Kingsborough Patent, New York, Loyalist, soldier of the Royal
Regiment of New York 1776-1783, settled in Charlottenburg,
Ontario. [DFpp]

FINLAYSON, JOHN, soldier of the Black Watch, land grant by the Nashwaak River, New Brunswick, 1785. [PANB:MC315]

FLEMING, JOHN, born in Scotland 1738, a planter in Fredericksburg, Virginia, militiaman of the Virginia Regiment 1757. [VMHB.1/2][L]

FLETCHER, ALEXANDER, former Captain of the 84th (Royal Highland Emigrants) Regiment, settled in Prince Edward Island after the Americam War, died in St John's 1793. [Scots Magazine.55.619]

FORBES, CHARLES, Captain of the 60th Regiment of Foot, died at Ticonderoga, New York, 1758. [Banff g/s]

FORBES, JAMES, soldier of the Black Watch, land grant by the Nashwaak River, New Brunswick, 1785. [PANB; MC315]

FORBES, JOHN, Dunfermline, Brigadier and Commander in Chief of the Expedition to Ohio and Fort Du Quesne 1758, died 1759. [SRO.RH15.38.81/83/112/120]

FORBES, JONATHAN, of Waterton, Colonel of St Catherine's Regiment, died in Jamaica 15.12.1820. [AJ#3815]

FORBES, THOMAS, Captain of Colonel Collingwood's Regiment of Foot, died in the West Indies 1703. [Pro.5/1158 PCC]

FORBES, WILLIAM, born in Scotland, a plasterer in King and Queen County, Virginia, a militiaman of the Virginia Regiment 1757. [VMHB.1/2][L]

FRASER, ALEXANDER, born in Scotland 1731, a planter in Culpepper County, Virginia, a militiaman of the Virginia Regiment 1757. [VMHB.1/2][L]

FRASER, ALEXANDER, born ca.1729, Lieutenant of the 78th [Fraser Highlanders] Regiment 1756-1763, settled in Quebec 1763, Captain of the 84th {Royal Highland Emigrants] Regiment 1779, died 1799. [McCord Museum, Montreal, #M17764]

FRASER, ARCHIBALD, Lieutenant and Paymaster of the 2nd West Indian Regiment, formerly of the 93rd Highland Regiment, died in Nassau, New Providence, 20.8.1826. [Edinburgh Advertiser]

FRASER, DANIEL, an officer of Fraser's Highlanders 1757-1763, later a merchant-skipper in Virginia 1763-1776, a Loyalist. [PRO.AO13.4.195]

FRASER, JAMES, born in Scotland 1730, a militiaman of the Virginia Regiment 1758. [VMHB.1/2][L]

FRASER, JAMES, born in Scotland 1733, a planter in King and Queen County, Virginia, a militiaman of the Virginia Regiment 1757. [VMHB.1/2][L]

FRASER, JAMES, born in the Scottish Highlands 1722, a militiaman of the Virginia Regiment 1757, [VMHB.1/2]

FRASER, JAMES, paymaster of the Royal Artillery in New York, 23.9.1782. [SRO.RS.Inverness#34]

FRASER, JAMES, born in Aird, Inverness-shire, a carpenter, to America 1775, 8 years a soldier of the 84th [Royal Highland Emigrants] Regiment, married Mary, daughter of Donald Cameron, settled in Strathmore, Nova Scotia, 1784. [SG.III.3.98]

FRASER, JOHN, born in Scotland 1737, a labourer in Cumberland County, Virginia, and a militiaman of the Virginia Regiment 1757. [VMHB.1/2][L]

FRASER, JOHN, Captain of the 78th (Fraser Highlander's Regiment), land grant in New York 26.8.1773. [PCCol.5.597]

FRASER, JOHN, soldier of the Black Watch, land grant by the Nashwaak River, New Brunswick, 1785. [PANB: MC315]

FRASER, Lieutenant MALCOLM, a reduced officer, applied for a land grant of 20,000 acres in Quebec 9.11.1764, [JCTP.1765.185; 1766.151]

FRASER, SIMON, born 1726, Lieutenant General of the 78th (Fraser Highlanders) Regiment 1757, fought at Louisbourg and Quebec, Major General, [ANY.1.20]; Colonel of the 78th Regiment, given a land grant in New York 1773. [ActsPCCol.V.598]; died 8.2.1782. [ANY.1.20]

FRASER, SIMON, born 1732, third son of Charles Fraser of Inverallochy, joined 78th{Fraser's Highlanders] Regiment in 1757, Captain, died at Quebec 15.10.1762. [ANY.1.20]

FRASER, THOMAS, Corporal of the Black Watch, wife and 2 children, land grant by the Nashwaak River, New Brunswick, 1785. [PANB: MC315]

FRASER, Captain, late of the 82nd Regiment, disbanded in Halifax, Nova Scotia, allocated 700 acres in Nova Scotia 1784. [HP115]

GARDINER, DAVID, born in Montrose 1786, Assistant Commissary General of the Forces, died in St John's, New Brunswick, 22.1.1827. [AJ#4135]

GARDNER, JOHN, soldier of the Black Watch, land grant by the Nashwaak River, New Brunswick, 1785. [PANB: MC315]

GEDDES, JOHN, born 1788, son of John Geddes and Margaret Anderson, assistant surgeon of the 54th Regiment, died in Jamaica 11.1808. [Bellie g/s]

GILLIES, ROBERT, officer in the American Provincial Corps, cnf 7.6.1783 Commissariot of Edinburgh [SRO.CC8.8.125]

GLENDENNING, DAVID, born in Scotland 1721, 5'10", deserted from the Virginia Regiment 11.8.1756. [Virginia Gazette#329]

GORDON, ALEXANDER, sergeant, allocated land grant of 200 acres at
Merrigonish, Nova Scotia, 1784. [ANQ.11.250]

GORDON, ALEXANDER, corporal, allocated 100 acres of land in
Pictou, Nova Scotia, 1784. [ANQ.II.250]

GORDON, AN(DREW), brother of Thomas Gordon of Duchray, officer
of the 42nd Highlanders 1762-, member of the St Andrew's Society
of New York 1762, lived on Broadway, New York, 1771.
[ANY.1.48]

GORDON, ARCHIBALD, born in Scotland, Colonel of the Pittsylvania
Company of the Virginia Militia 1774, died in Franklin County.
[VMHB.VII.9/16]

GORDON, JAMES, late Captain of the Aberdeenshire Militia, died in
Port Maria, Jamaica, 20.11.1820. [AJ#3818]

GOULD, WILLIAM, from Glasgow, Lieutenant of the 5th West Indian
Regiment, died in Belize 11.5.1801. [Gentleman's Magazine,
72.181]

GRAEME, CHARLES. Captain in the Royal American Regiment 1779,
son of Thomas Graeme of Balgowan. [SRO.SC49.57.4]

GRAHAM. JAMES, late of the 64th Regiment, died in Charleston, South
Carolina, 1802. [Scots Magazine: 64.708]

GRAHAM, JOHN, Captain Lieutenant of the 42nd Foot, killed at Bushy
Run 6.8.1763. [AJ#824]

GRAHAM, JOHN, Captain of the 42nd Foot, wounded at Bushy Run
6.8.1763. [AJ#822]

GRANT, ALEXANDER, emigrated to America 1773, settled on the
Kingsborough Patent, New York, Loyalist, soldier of the Royal
Regiment of New York, settled in Cornwall, Ontario. [DFpp]

GRANT, Colonel JAMES, Governor of East Florida, 1770s.
[SRO.RS29.VIII.202, 203, 362, 364]

GRANT, JOHN, Commisary of Ordnance in New York, cnf 23.5.1789
Commissariot of Edinburgh

GRANT, PATRICK, emigrated from Greenock to Boston on the Glasgow
Packet, Captain Alexander Porterfield, in September 1775, enlisted
into the 84th (Royal Highland Emigrants) Regiment 23 October
1775. [SRO.GD174.2093]

GRANT, PETER, emigrated to America 1774, settled on the
Kingsborough Patent, New York, Loyalist, soldier of the Royal
Regiment of New York, settled in Charlottenburgh, Ontario.
[DFpp]

GRANT, WILLIAM, a former Lieutenant of the 42nd Regiment, wife his
wife and family, emigrated from Mull to New York on the Moore

of Greenock, master MacLarty, 12.7.1774. [Scots Magazine:36:446]

GRAY, JOHN, youngest son of William Gray of Lairg, Sutherland, to Georgia 1746 as Ensign of Oglethorpe's Regiment, later Ensign of Mackay's Independent Company in America, land grant in Georgia 1759, pro.22.8.1770 PCC. [SG.XLI.2]

GRAY, JOHN, soldier of the Black Watch, land grant by the Nashwaak River, New Brunswick, 1785. [PANB:MC315]

GRAY, THOMAS, born in Edinburgh 1719, a labourer and a drummer, deserted from Captain R. Hodgson's Independent Company in Virginia 6.1746. {'Wanted' notice}. [Virginia Gazette #518]

GRIERSON, JAMES, settled in Augusta, Georgia, Loyalist, Captain of Militia 1773. [PRO.AO.13.35.247/258]

GUNN, ALEXANDER, soldier of the Black Watch, land grant by the Nashwaak River, New Brunswick, 1785. [PANB: MC315]

GUNN, JAMES, soldier of the Black Watch, land grant by the Nashwaak River, New Brunswick, 1785. [PANB: MC315]

HAGGART, WILLIAM, Ensign of 77th Montgomery's Highlanders 6.1.1757, Lieutenant 16.9.1758, Quartermaster 16.8.1762, member of the St Andrew's Society of New York 1762. [ANY.1.49]

HAMILTON, JOHN, born in Dumfries, Scotland, a labourer, deserted from Lieutenant Fleming at Suffolk, Virginia, 24.9.1754. [Virginia Gazette#248]

HARDINE, ALEXANDER, possibly from Edinburgh, Lieutenant Colonel of Gouch's Regiment, died in Carthagena, PCC Admin. 25.2.1743, Prob.3/42/17

HARRISON, JOSEPH, in Brownfield, Glasgow, Quartermaster of the Loyal American Regiment, cnf 3.9.1804 Commissariot of Glasgow. [SRO.CC9.7.76.6]

HAZEL, DAVID, born in Scotland 1731, a planter in Stafford County, Virginia, a militiaman of the Virginia Regiment 1757. [VMHB.1/2][L]

HENDERSON, THOMAS, son of Reverend Thomas Henderson and Rachel Kinnaird, surgeon of the 90th Regiment, died in Havanna 7.1762. [Skirling g/s]

HOSACK, ALEXANDER, born in Elgin 1728, son of Alexander Hosack and Margaret Cook, a soldier in the French and Indian Wars, later settled in New York as a merchant during 1763, died in Hackensack, New York, 9.1.1826. [Bio.Reg. of the St Andrew's Society of New York.1.206]

HOME, WALTER, born 4.10.1742, son of Reverend William Home in Fogo, Berwickshire, Colonel of the 42nd Regiment, served through the American War of Independence, dead by 27.2.1800. [F.2.16]

INGLIS, JAMES, Lieutenant of the Maryland Loyalists, son of Thomas Inglis feuar in Clackmannan, cnf 6.12.1785 Commissariot of Edinburgh

KENNEDY, DAVID, born in Scotland 1733, a militiaman of the Virginia Regiment 1756. [VMHB.1/2][L]

KENNEDY, HUGH, soldier of the Black Watch, land grant by the Nashwaak River, New Brunswick, 1785. [PANB: MC315]

KENNEDY, JOHN, soldier of the Black Watch, land grant by the Nashwaak River, New Brunswick, 1785. [PANB: MC315]

KENNISS, ANDREW, born in Scotland 1734, a carpenter in Spotsylvania County, Virginia, a militiaman of the Virginia Regiment 1757. [VMHB.1/2][L]

KIRKLAND, JOHN, born in Scotland 1735, a planter in Northumberland County, Virginia, a militiaman of the Virginia Regiment 1756. [VMHB.1/2][L]

LAMONT, NORMAN, Captain of the 89th Regiment of Highlanders, 1760; Major of the 55th Regiment of Foot, Philadelphia 1777. [Laing Charters, #3210/3244]

LANDELLS, JAMES, Lieutenant of the 60th Regiment, son of Reverend James Landells in Coldingham, died in Port Antonio, Jamaica, 1803. [AJ#2915]

LESLIE, DANIEL, born in Scotland 1728, a planter and a militiaman of the Virginia Regiment 1755. [VNHB.1/2][L]

LESSLY, GEORGE, soldier of the Black Watch, land grant by the Nashwaak River, New Brunswick, 1785. [PANB: MC315]

LINDSAY, CHARLES STEWART, Captain of the South Carolina Royalists in the American War, later Lieutenant in the Fifeshire Militia, died in Dundee 19.1.1813. [AJ#3398]

LINDSAY, JOHN, from Wormiston, Fife, settled in Cherry Valley, Oswego County, New York, 1729, Captain of the local independent company and Lieutenant Governor of Oswego, died 1751. [SRO.GD203.11.14]

LOGIE, WILLIAM, son of Alexander Logie in Fochabers, (1756-1836), and Agnes Cluny, (1757-1823), a Major in US Army. [Speymouth g/s]

LOURIE, JOHN, born in Scotland 1735, a joiner in Essex County, Virginia, and a militiaman of the Virginia Regiment 1757. [VMHB.1/2][L]

LYLE, JAMES, born in Scotland 1733, a carpenter in Williamsburg, Virginia, and a militiaman of the Virginia Regiment 1757. [VMHB.1/2][L]

MCARTHUR, DUNCAN, emigrated from Greenock to Boston on the Glasgow Packet, Captain Arthur Porterfield, in September 1775, emlisted in the 84th (Royal Highland Emigrants) Regiment 23 October 1775. [SRO.GD174.2093]

MCBAIN, ANGUS, soldier of the Black Watch, land grant by the Nashwaak River, New Brunswick, 1785. [PANB: MC315]

MCCASKILL, JOHN, born 1758, soldier of the 42nd Regiment, died in battle in the West Indies 6.6.1796. [Eynort, Skye, g/s]

MCCLENNAN, JOHN, emigrated to America 1773, settled on the Kingsborough Patent, New York, soldier of the 2nd Battalion the Royal Regiment of New York, settled in Charlottenburgh, Ontario. [DFpp]

MCCLOUD, WILLIAM, born in Scotland 1730, a militiaman of the Virginia Regiment 1756. [VMHB.1/2][L]

MCCULLOCH, R.D., drummer of the Black Watch. land grant by the Nashwaak River, New Brunswick, 1785. [PANB:MC315]

MCCULLOCH, WILLIAM, drummer of the Black Watch, land grant by the Nashwaak River, New Brunswick, 1785. [PANB:MC315]

MCDONALD, ALEXANDER, Arnamurchan, Lieutenant of the 77th (Montgomery's Highlanders) Regiment 1756-1763, wounded on the expedition to Fort Duquesne, settled as a merchant in New York, member of the St Andrew's Society of New York 1767, Loyalist in 1776, Captain of the 84th (Royal Highland Emigrants), later in Halifax, Nova Scotia. [ANY.1.65]

MACDONALD, ALEXANDER, born 1762, son of Alexander MacDonald and Helen McNab, emigrated to New York 1773, Loyalist, officer in Butler's Rangers, died 18.3.1842. [CD.3.359]

MACDONALD, ALEXANDER, son of Alexander MacDonald of Keppoch and Jessie Stewart, Major in the Glengarry Fencibles, settled in Keppoch, Prince Edward Island, died 12.1809. [CD.3.422]

MACDONALD, ALEXANDER, of Aberchalder, son of John MacDonald and Mary MacDonald, settled in Charlottenburg, Canada, before 1776, Loyalist, Captain in the King's Royal Regiment of New York, died 1787. [CD.3.353]

MCDONALD, ALEXANDER, sr., soldier of the Black Watch, wife, land grant by the Nashwaak River, New Brunswick, 1785. [PANB:MC315]

MCDONALD, ALEXANDER, soldier of the Black Watch, land grant by the Nashwaak River, New Brunswick, 1785. [PANB: MC315]

MCDONALD, ANGUS, born in Scotland 1735, a seaman in King George County, Virginia, a militiaman of the Virginia Regiment 1757. [VMHB.1/2][L]

MCDONALD, CHARLES, Captain of the 78th Regiment, killed at Signet Hill 15.9.1763. [SRO.GD21.486]

MCDONALD, DONALD, soldier of the Black Watch, land grant by the Nashwaak River, New Brunswick, 1785. [PANB: MC315]

MCDONALD, DONALD, of Lochmoidart, Lieutenant Colonel of the 2nd Royals, died in Tobago 1804. [AJ#2652]

MCDONALD, JAMES, soldier of the Black Watch, land grant by the Nashwaak River, New Brunswick, 1785. [PANB: MC315]

MCDONALD, JOHN, born in Scotland 1734, a planter in Caroline County, Virginia, a militiaman in the Virginia Regiment 1756. [VMHB.1/2][L]

MCDONALD, JOHN, soldier of the Black Watch, land grant by the Nashwaak River, New Brunswick, 1785. [PANB: MC315]

MCDONALD, LAUGHLIN, born in the Highlands, a soldier of Loudoun's Highlanders at Boston 1757, at Louisbourg 1758, at the Plains of Abraham and at the Siege of Quebec, also fought under Admiral Hawke in the West Indies, died in Belfast, USA, 25.8.1821. [Scotsman.5.247]

MCDONELL, AENEAS, late Captain of the 6th Royal Veterans, died in Nelson, Miramachi, 10.3.1828. [AJ#4205]

MCDONELL, ALLEN, born in Lundie, Inverness-shire, emigrated to America 1773, settled on the Kingsborough Patent, New York, Loyalist, Captain of the 1st Battalion of the Royal Regiment of New York, settled in Matilda Township, Glengarry County, Ontario. [DFpp]

MCDONELL, ARCHIBALD, born in Scotland, settled on the Kingsborough Patent, New York, Loyalist, possibly a Lieutenant of the 84th {Royal Highland Emigrants} Regiment, later Lieutenant Colonel of the 1st Regiment of the Prince Edward Island Militia. [DFpp]

MCDONELL, DUNCAN, born in Glen Moriston, Inverness-shire, settled on the Kingsborough Patent, New York, Loyalist, soldier of the 2nd Battalion of the Royal Regiment of New York, settled in Cornwall, Ontario. [DFpp]

MCDONELL, DUNCAN, emigrated to America 1773, settled on the Kingsborough Patent, New York, soldier of the Royal Regiment of New York and in the 84th Regiment, settled in Cornwall, Ontario. [DFpp]

MCDONELL, JOHN, jr., of Loch Garry, Captain of the 78th {Fraser's Highlanders} Regiment 13.1.1757, wounded at the Heights of Abraham, Major of the 71st Fraser's Highlanders, member of the St Andrew's Society of New York 1759, Colonel of the 76th McDonald's Highlanders, died 1789. [ANY.1.32]

MCDONELL, JOHN, Collachie, Inverness-shire, emigrated to America 1773, settled on the Kingsborough Patent, New York, Loyalist, soldier of the 84th {Royal Highland Emigrants} Regiment, settled in the Eastern District, Ontario. [DFpp]

MCDONELL, JOHN, Auchengleen, Inverness-shire, emigrated to America 1773, settled on the Kingsborough Patent, New York, soldier of the 84th {Royal Highland Emigrants} Regiment 1776-1783, settled in New Johnstown, Cornwall, Ontario. [DFpp]

MCDONELL, JOHN, born in Dalechreggan, Inverness-shire, emigrated to America 1773, settled on the Kingsborough Patent, New York, Loyalist, soldier of the 1st Battalion of the Royal Regiment of New York, settled in Canada. [DFpp]

MCDONELL, JOHN, born at Fort Augustus, Inverness-shire, emigrated to America 1773, settled on the Kingsborough Patent, New York, soldier of the 1st Battalion of the Royal Regiment of New York, died 1786. [DFpp]

MCDONELL, JOHN, Inveroucht, Inverness-shire, emigrated to America 1773, settled on the Kingsborough Patent, New York, Loyalist, soldier of the 2nd Battalion of the Royal Regimne tof New York, settled at River aux Raisins, Ontario. [DFpp]

MCDONELL, JOHN, born in Baldron, Inverness-shire, emigrated to America 1774, settled on the Kingsborough Patent, New York, Loyalist, soldier of the Royal Regiment of New York, settled in Charlottenburgh, Ontario. [DFpp]

MCDONELL, JOHN, of Leek, Loch Oich, Inverness-shire, Jacobite soldier in 1745, Lieutenant of the 78th Regiment during French and Indian War 1756-1763, wounded at Louisbourg 1758, emigrated from Fort William, Scotland to America 1773, settled on the Kingsborough Patent, New York, Loyalist, Captain of the 84th {Royal Highland Emigrants}, died 11.11.1782 buried in Montreal. [DFpp][PC.Col.5.597]

MCDONELL, KENNETH, emigrated to America 1773, settled on the Kingsborough Patent, New York, Loyalist, sergeant of the 84th {Royal Highland Regiment}, settled in Cornwall, Ontario. [DFpp]

MCDONELL, RONALD, son of Keppoch, Lieutenant of the 78ht Fraser's Highlamders 14.1.1757, Captain 17.10.1759, member of the St Andrew's Society of New York 1759. [ANY.1.32]

MCDONELL, RANOLD, of Ardnabee, Jacobite soldier 1745-1746, soldier of the 17th Regiment, then of the 60th{Royal Americans} Regiment, settled on the Kingsborough Patent, New York, 1773, Loyalist, soldier of the 84th {Royal Highland Emigrants} and later of the 2nd Battalion of the Royal Canadian Volunteers. [DFpp]

MCDOUGALL, DONALD, soldier of the Black Watch, wife, land grant by the Nashwaak River, New Brunswick, 1785. [PANB: MC315]

MCDOUGALL, DUNCAN, emigrated from Greenock to Boston on the Glasgow Packet, Captain Arthur Porterfield, in September 1775, emlisted in the 84th (Royal Highland Emigrants) Regiment 23 October 1775. [SRO.GD174.2093]

MCDOUGALL. GEORGE, former Lieutenant of the Royal American Regiment, settled on Hog Island, Detroit, 1761. [PC.Col.5.119]

MCFADDIN, DONALD, soldier of the Black Watch, land grant by the Nashwaak River, New Brunswick, 1785. [PANB: MC315]

MCFAIN, DANIEL, born in Scotland 1730, a planter in Winchester, Virginia, a militiaman of the Virginia Regiment 1756. [VMHB.1/2][L]

MCGILLIS, DONALD, born in Muneraghie, Inverness-shire, emigrated to America 1773, settled on the Kingsborough Patent, New York, sergeant of the Royal Regiment of New York 1777-1783, settled in Williamstown, Charlottenburg, Ontario. [DFpp]

MCGILLVRAY, ALEXANDER, soldier of the Black Watch, land grant by the Nashwaak River, New Brunswick, 1785. [PANB: MC315]

MCGREGOR, DUNCAN, soldier of the Black Watch, land grant by the Nashwaak River, New Brunswick, 1785. [PANB: MC315]

MCGREGOR, JOHN, soldier of the Black Watch, land grant by the Nashwaak River, New Brunswick, 1785. [PANB: MC315]

MCGREGOR, MALCOLM, soldier of the Black Watch, land grant by the Nashwaak River, New Brunswick, 1785. [PANB: MC315]

MCGRUER, DONALD, emigrated to America 1773, settled on the Kingsborough Patent, New York, Loyalist, soldier of then84th {Royal Highland Emigrants} Regiment, died at Sorel. [DFpp]

MCGRUER, JOHN, emigrated to America 1763, settled on Kingsborough Patent, New York, 1770, Loyalist, corporal of the Royal Regiment of New York 1777, settled in Charlottenburg, Ontario. [DFpp]

MCHARD, PETER, born in Scotland 1761, American Army officer,
   captured at Ligonier 25.4.1779, a prisoner at Fort Chambly. [British
   Library, Haldemand Papers, Add.M.S.21483, 79.281.1/3]
MCINTOSH, AENEAS, Captain at Parachocock 20.4.1738. [GA.Council
   Rec.3.427]
MCINTOSH, ALEXANDER, soldier of the Black Watch, wife and child,
   land grant by the Nashwaak River, New Brunswick, 1785. [PANB:
   MC315]
MCINTOSH, JOHN, born 24.3.1700 son of Lachlan McIntosh and Mary
   Lockhart in Badenoch, to Georgia on the Prince of Wales 10.1735,
   Captain of the Highland Company there 1738, died 9.1761.
   [GA.Council Rec.3.427][GHQ.LVII.1]
MCINTOSH, JOHN, emigrated to America 1773, settled on the
   Kingsborough Patent, New York, soldier of the84th Regiment
   1776-1783, settled on River aux Raisins. [DFpp]
MCINTOSH, LACHLAN, born 1726, Revolutionary General, died
   19.2.1806. [Savannah Death Register]
MCINTOSH, LACHLAN, drummer of the Black Watch, land grant by the
   Nashwaak River, New Brunswick, 1785. [PANB: MC315]
MCINTOSH, MALCOLM, soldier of the Black Watch, land grant by the
   Nashwaak River, New Brunswick, 1785. [PANB: MC315]
MCINTOSH, WILLIAM, Sergeant of the Black Watch, wife and 2
   children, land grant by the Nashwaak River, New Brunswick, 1785.
   [PANB:MC315]
MCINTYRE, ...., Ranger Captain at Fort Prince George, Georgia, 1738.
   [GA.Council Rec.10.5.1738]
MCINTYRE, DANIEL, born in Scotland 1734, a planter in
   Fredericksburg, Virginia, a militiaman of the Virginia Regiment
   1756. [VMHB1/2][L]
MCIVER, ALEXANDER, soldier of the Black Watch, land grant by the
   Nashwaak River, New Brunswick, 1785. [PANB: MC315]
MCKAY, ANGUS, emigrated to America 1772, settled on the
   Kingsborough Patent, New York, 1773, Loyalist, soldier of the
   Royal Regiment of New York, settled in Glengarry County,
   Ontario. [DFpp]
MCKAY, ANGUS, soldier of the Black Watch, land grant by the
   Nashwaak River, New Brunswick, 1785. [PANB: MC315]
MCKAY, CHARLES, born 1718, to Georgia 1735, Officer of the
   Independent Highland Company there.
   [SG.XLI.I][PRO.CO5.668.130/1] [PC.Col.6.498]

MCKAY, DONALD, emigrated to America 1773, settled on the Kingsborough Patent, New York, Loyalist, soldier of the 1st Battalion of the Royal Regiment of New York, settled on River aux Raisins, Ontario. [DFpp]⁻

MACKAY, DONALD, Tain, Ross-shire, Sergeant of the 76th Regiment, discharged 1.11.1783, settled in Shelbourne, Nova Scotia. [SG.VIII.4.23]

MCKAY, HENRY, soldier of the Black Watch, land grant by the Nashwaak River, New Brunswick, 1785. [PANB:MS315]

MCKAY, HUGH, Lieutenant in Georgia, 1738. [PRO.CO5.668]

MCKAY, JOHN, soldier of the Black Watch, land grant by the Nashwaak River, New Brunswick, 1785. [PANB: MC315]

MCKAY, JOHN, from Bettyhill, Sutherland, a Captain of the 27th Regiment, married Amelia Isabella de Wolff, daughter of Benjamin de Wolff in Windsor, Nova Scotia, 1821. [Blackwood's Edinburgh Magazine #10.489]

MCKAWLEY, WILLIAM, soldier of the Black Watch, land grant by the Nashwaak River, New Brunswick, 1785. [PANB:MC315]

MCKAY, DONALD, soldier of the Black Watch, land grant by the Nashwaak River, New Brunswick, 1785. [PANB: MC315]

MCKAY, DUNCAN, soldier of the Black Watch, land grant by the Nashwaak River, New Brunswick, 1785. [PANB: MC315]

MCKAY, FRANCIS, soldier of the Black Watch, land grant by the Nashwaak River, New Brunswick, 1785. [PANB:MC315]

MCKAY, GEORGE, sr., soldier of the Black Watch, land grant by the Nashwaak River, New Brunswick, 1785. [PANB: MC315]

MCKAY, GEORGE, jr., soldier of the Black Watch, land grant by the Nashwaak River, New Brunswick, 1785. [PANB: MC315]

MACKAY, HUGH, son of Roderick Mackay and Isobel Gray in Clashneach of Durnes, arrived in Georgia 1736, Officer of Oglethorpe's Regiment, later Captain of the Highland troop of Rangers, died 1743. [SG.XLI.1]

MACKAY, JAMES, to Georgia 1735, Officer of Oglethorpe's Regiment and Commander of an Independent Company of Foot in South Carolina 1736-1755, died in Alexandria, Georgia, 1780s. [SG.XLI.1]

MCKAY, JOHN, Bettyhill, Sutherland, Captain of the 27th Regiment of Foot, married Amelia Isabella, third daughter of Benjamin de Wolff, in Windsor, Nova Scotia, 1821. [Scotsman.5.249]

MACKAY, PATRICK, of Sidera and Scourie, Sutherland, son of Captain
Hugh Mackay of Borley and Jane Dunbar, to Georgia 1732,
Captain of an Independent Company there 1734-35, pro. 1777 S.C.
[SG.XLI.1][PRO.CO5.646.C9; CO5.640.45; CO5.668][BM294]

MCKAY, ROBERT, sr., soldier of the Black Watch, land grant by the
Nashwaak River, New Brunswick, 1785. [PANB: MC315]

MCKAY, ROBERT, soldier of the Black Watch, land grant by the
Nashwaak River, New Brunswick, 1785. [PANB: MC315]

MCKAY, ROBERT, jr., soldier of the Black Watch, wife and 3 children,
land grant by the Nashwaak River, New Brunswick, 1785. [PANB:
MC315]

MACKAY, SAMUEL, born 1722, to Georgia, Officer of Oglethorpe's
Regiment 1742-49, Officer of an Independent Company 1749-1761.
[SG.XLI.1]

MACKAY, SAMUEL, Ensign of the 2nd Battalion of the King's Royal
Regiment of New York, 1782. [Musee du Quebec, #A-54.282D]

MCKAY, WILLIAM, soldier of the Black Watch, wife and child, land
grant by the Nashwaak River, New Brunswick, 1785. [PANB:
MC315]

MCKENZIE, ALEXANDER, soldier of the Black Watch, land grant by
the Nashwaak River, New Brunswick, 1785. [PANB:MC315]

MCKENZIE, HUGH, soldier of the Black Watch, land grant by the
Nashwaak River, New Brunswick, 1785. [PANB:MC315]

MACKENZIE, DAVID, Lieutenant of the Royal American Regiment, son
of David MacKenzie a shipmaster in Inverness, cnf 11.1.1776
Edinburgh

MCKENZIE, JOHN, soldier of the Black Watch, land grant by the
Nashwaak River, New Brunswick, 1785. [PANB: MC315]

MCKENZIE, JOHN, soldier of the Black Watch, land grant by the
Nashwaak River, New Brunswick, 1785. [PANB: MC315]

MACKENZIE, JOHN, Sergeant of the Black Watch, land grant by the
Nashwaak River, New Brunswick, 1785. [PANB:MC315]

MCKENZIE, RODERICK, Captain of the 77th Regiment, killed at
Quide Vide 13.9.1762. [SRO.GD21.486]

MCKENZIE, RODERICK, soldier of the Black Watch, land grant by the
Nashwaak River, New Brunswick, 1785. [PANB: MC315]

MCKENZIE, RODERICK, born 1784, Major in the 77th Regiment, died
in Jamaica 3.1.1825. [AJ#4027]

MCKENZIE, ....., Corporal of the Black Watch, wife and 3 children, land
grant on the Nashwaak River, New Brunswick, 1785. [PANB:
MC315]

MACKIE, GEORGE, sixth son of William Mackie in Ormiston, East
Lothian, as Ensign of the 72nd Gordon Highlanders fought in
Portugal, Spain, and at Waterloo, Lieutenant and Adjutant of the
92nd Highlanders, died at Up Park Camp, Jamaica. [Edinburgh
Magazine:11.1819]

MCKINNON, RANALD, born in Skye 1737, Ensign of the 77th
Montgomery's Highlanders, served at Fort DuQuesne, wounded by
Cherokee, a Lieutenant at the recapture of St John's,
Newfoundland, 2000 acre land grant in Nova Scotia, Colonel of
Militia in Argyle, Nova Scotia, 1775, Captain of the 2nd Battalion
the Royal Highland Emigrants (Light Company) 14.6.1775, served
in Nova Scotia and with Clinton's Grand Army in the South, settled
in Nova Scotia after 1783, died 28.4.1805. [JAHR.73.234/5,290]

MCLAGAN, PETER, Corporal of the Black Watch, land grant by the
Nashwaak River, New Brunswick, 1785. [PANB: MC315]

MCLAINE, MURDOCH, emigrated from Greenock to Boston on the
Glasgow Packet, Captain Arthur Porterfield, in September 1775,
enlisted in the 84th (Royal Highland Emigrants) Regiment 23
October 1775. [SRO.GD174.2093]

MCLEAN, ALLAN, born in Torloisk, Mull, 1725, officer of the Scots
Brigade in Dutch Service, then in 1756 Lieutenant of the 62nd
[Royal Americans] - wounded at Ticonderoga 1758, Captain of an
Independent Company 1759 - present at Niagara; at the Siege of
Quebec, Commander of the 114th Foot ( Royal Highland
Volunteers) 1761, [ANY.1.10]; Lieutenant Colonel of the 78th
Highlanders, given a land grant in New York 1773.
[ActsPCCol.V.598]; Loyalist in 1776, Lieutenant Colonel of the
84th (Royal Highland Emigrants) Regiment, Brigadier General and
military governor of Quebec 1777, died in London 1797.
[ANY.1.10]

MCLEAN, ARCHIBALD, Captain of the 56th Regiment, died in St
Domingo 20.1.1798. [AJ#2621]

MCLEAN, DONALD, emigrated to America 1773, settled on the
Kingsborough Patent, New York, Loyalist, soldier of the Royal
Regiment of New York, settled in Charlottenburg, Ontario. [DFpp]

MCLEAN, DUNCAN, officer of the 2nd West Indian Regiment, cnf 1825
Commissariot of Edinburgh [SRO.SC70.1.33]

MCLEAN, FRANCIS, Lieutenant Colonel of the 78th Regiment, land
grant in New York 1773. [PCCol.V.598]

MCLEAN, HECTOR, emigrated from Greenock to Boston on the Glasgow Packet, Captain Arthur Porterfield, in September 1775, enlisted in the 84th (Royal Highland Emigrants) Regiment 23 October 1775. [SRO.GD174.2093]

MACLEAN, JOHN, born 15.4.1752 son of Reverend Alexander MacLean and Christina MacLean in Mull, an American Army Officer, died in Halifax, Nova Scotia. [F.4.115]

MCLEAN, JOHN, Lieutenant of the 2nd Battalion of the Royal Highland Emigrants, cnf 31.5.1783 Commissariat of Edinburgh

MCLEAN, LAUCHLIN, born in Scotland 1733, a planter in Prince William County, Virginia, a militiaman of the Virginia Regiment 1757. [VMHB.1/2][L]

MCLEAN, LACHLAN, emigrated from Greenock to Boston on the Glasgow Packet, Captain Arthur Porterfield, in September 1775, enlisted into the 84th(Royal Highland Emigrants) Regiment 23 October 1775. [SRO.GD174.2093]

MCLEAN, MURDOCH, officer of the West Indian Regiment, cnf 6.1.1797 Commissariot of Edinburgh. [SRO.CC8.8.130]

MCLEAN, ......, Corporal of the Black Watch, wife and 3 children, land grant by the Nashwaak River, New Brunswick, 1785. [PANB: MC315]

MCLEOD, ALEXANDER, Major in the North Carolina Highlanders, died 2.1797. [Old Dunvegan g/s]

MCLEOD, DONALD, Corporal of the Black Watch, wife, land grant by the Nashwaak River, New Brunswick, 1785. [PANB: MC315]

MCLEOD, DUNCAN, soldier of the Black Watch, land grant by the Nashwaak River, New Brunswick, 1785. [PANB: MC315]

MCLEOD, JOHN, soldier of the Black Watch, land grant by the Nashwaak River, New Brunswick, 1785. [PANB: MC315]

MCLEOD, MALCOLM, soldier of the Black Watch, land grant by the Nashwaak River, New Brunswick, 1785. [PANB: MC315]

MCLEOD, MURDOCH, born in Scotland 1723, a planter in Westmoreland County, Virginia, a militiaman of the Virginia Regiment 1757. [VMHB.1/2][L]

MCLEOD, MURDOCH, soldier of the Black Watch, land grant on the Nashwaak River, New Brunswick, 1785. [PANB: MC315]

MCLEOD, NORMAN, Ensign of the 42nd Highlanders 1.1756, served in Nova Scotia under Lord Loudoun, fought under General Abercromby at Ticonderoga 1758, member of the St Andrew's Society of New York 1759, with Amherst to Lake Champlain and down the St Lawrence 1759-1760, Captain-Lieutenant of the 80th{Gage's Light Infantry} 1760-1763, Commissary at Niagara

1763-, Lieutenant of the 42nd Regiment 1775, Captain in the 71st
Regiment 1779, wounded in the Charleston campaign 1780,
surrendered with Cornwallis 1781. [ANY.1.33]

MCLEOD, ROBERT, soldier of the Black Watch, land grant by the
Nashwaak River, New Brunswick, 1785. [PANB: MC315]

MCLEOD, RODERICK, sr., soldier of the Black Watch, land grant by the
Nashwaak River, New Brunswick, 1785. [PANB: MC315]

MCLEOD, RODERICK, jr., wife and 2 children, soldier of the Black
Watch, land grant on the Nashwaak River, New Brunswick, 1785.
[PANB: MC315]

MCLEOD, WILLIAM, soldier of the Black Watch, land grant by the
Nashwaak River, New Brunswick, 1785. [PANB: MC315]

MCMILLAN, DONALD, soldier of the 84th [Royal Highland Emigrant]
Regiment, settled in Nova Scotia 1783. [PANS.MG100, vol.184,
#22]

MCMILLAN, MILES, soldier of the Black Watch, wife and 3 children,
land grant by the Nashwaak River, New Brunswick, 1785. [PANB:
MC315]

MCNABB, JAMES, Sergeant of the Black Watch, land grant by the
Nashwaak River, New Brunswick, 1785. [PANB:MC315]

MCNAUGHTON, ALEXANDER, settled in Wolfsboro, New Hampshire,
before 1776, a Loyalist soldier in the 84th [Royal Highland
Emigrant] Regiment, settled in Halifax, Nova Scotia, 1784.
[PRO.AO26.277-279]

MCNICOLL, DONALD, Lieutenant of the 88th Regiment of Foot,
31.2.1774, later Captain of the 84th {Royal Highland Emigrant}
Regiment 19.8.1780. [SRO.RS10.Argyll.11.114; 2.29]

MCPHARLAN, GEORGE, soldier of the Black Watch, land grant by the
Nashwaak River, New Brunswick, 1785. [PANB: MC315]

MCPHARLAN, JOHN, Sergeant of the Black Watch, wife, land grant by
the Nashwaak River, New Brunswick, 1785. [PANB: MC315]

MCPHERSON, Captain JOHN, of Philadelphia, Pennsylvania, late
commander of HM man o' war Britannia, admitted as a burgess of
Edinburgh by right of his father, 15.8.1764. [Roll of Edinburgh
Burgesses]

MCPHERSON, WILLIAM, born in Scotland 1737, a planter in
Goochland County, Virginia, a militiaman of the Virginia Regiment
1757. [VMHB.1/2][l]

MCPHERSON, WILLIAM, soldier of the Black Watch, wife, land grant
by the Nashwaak River, New Brunswick, 1785. [PANB: MC315]

MACPHERSON, ..., Ranger Captain at Fort Argyle, Georgia, 1738.
[GA.Council Rec.10.5.1738]

MCQUARRIE, HECTOR, emigrated from Greenock to Boston on the Glasgow Packet, Captain Arthur Porterfield, in September 1775, enlisted in the 84th(Royal Highland Emigrants) Regiment 23 October 1775. [SRO.GD174.2093]

MCRAW, DUNCAN, soldier of the Black Watch, land grant by the Nashwaak River, New Brunswick, 1785. [PANB: MC315]

MCRAW, FARQUHAR, soldier of the Black Watch, land grant by the Nashwaak River, New Brunswick, 1785. [PANB: MC315]

MCRAW, NIEL, soldier of the Black Watch, land grant by the Nashwaak River, New Brunswick, 1785. [PANB: MC315]

MCSWEEN, MURDOCH, soldier of the Black Watch, land grant by the Nashwaak River, New Brunswick, 1785. [PANB: MC315]

MAITLAND, Hon. ALEXANDER, son of the Earl of Lauderdale, officer of the 1st Battalion of the 71st (Fraser's Highlanders), fought in New Jersey and Pennsylvania 1776-1777, led expedition to Savannah 12.1777, died there. [ANY.1.66]

MAITLAND, Hon.RICHARD, born 1724, fourth son of the Earl of Lauderdale, officer of the 43rd Regiment 1754, fought under Wolfe at Quebec 1762, member of the St Andrew's Society of New York 1764, Colonel 1772, died 13.7.1772, buried in Trinity Church Yard, New York. [ANY.1.57]

MALCOLM, WILLIAM, born in Aberdeen 1750, settled in New York by 1763, member of the St Andrew's Society of New York 1763, Colonel of the 2nd (Malcolm's) Regiment, Colonel of the 16th Additional Continental Regiment, Deputy Adjutant General under General Gates, Brigadier-General of Militia in New York and Richmond Counties, died 1.9.1791. [ANY.1.34]

MALLOCH, DONALD, soldier in the 74th Argyll Highlanders during the American War of Independence, stationed at Fort George, Maine, discharged and settled in St Andrews, New Brunswick, 1783. [SG.30.2.65]

MASTERTON, JOHN, soldier of the Black Watch, land grant by the Nashwaak River, New Brunswick, 1785. [PANB: MC315]

MATTHEWSON, ALEXANDER, Sergeant of the Black Watch, land grant by the Nashwaak River, New Brunswick, 1785. [PANB:MC315]

MATTHEWSON, GEORGE, soldier of the Black Watch, land grant by the Nashwaak River, New Brunswick, 1785. [PANB: MC315]

MERCER, HUGH, born 16.1.1726, son of Rev. William Mercer and Ann Munro in Pitsligo, Aberdeenshire, a physician and soldier, educated at King's College, Aberdeen, 1744, Jacobite, emigrated from Leith to Philadelphia 1746, settled in Greencastle, King George County, Virginia, married Isabel Gordon, father of Anne, John, William, George and Hugh, Revolutionary General, died at Battle of Princeton, New Jersey, pro.20.3.1777 Spotsylvania County, Virginia. [KCA.2.315][Spotsylvania Deeds E169][WMQ.2.22.97]

MERCER, JAMES, of Clevage, born 16.7.1725 son of Reverend James Mercer and Elizabeth Logan, Lieutenant in the 48th Regiment of Foot, died in Albany, New York, 11.1757. [F.4.194][SM.19.614]

MERCER, Colonel JAMES FRANCIS, son of Reverend Laurence Mercer and Jean Lindsay in Gask, died at Fort Oswego 13.8.1756. [F.4.274]

MERCER, ROBERT, of the New York Militia 1777. [SRO.GD90.II.245.2]

MILLER, WILLIAM, army deserter in Virginia 1777. [Va.Gaz.19.9.1777]

MILNE, DAVID, Lieutenant of the 42nd Regiment 19.7.1757, wounded at Ticonderoga 1758, member of the St Andrew's Society of New York 1759, wounded at Martinique 1762. [ANY.1.34]

MILLS, THOMAS, soldier of the 55th Regiment, discharged in Halifax, Nova Scotia, 1765, a carman in New York, Loyalist, settled in Halifax, Nova Scotia, 1784. [PRO.AO13.14.358/362]

MONRO, Lieutenant General WILLIAM HECTOR, born 1769, Governor of Trinidad, died in Bath 3.1.1821. [Great Canford g/s, Dorset]

MORRISON, ALEXANDER, born 1717, former Captain of the North Carolina Highlanders, died in Greenock 28.1.1805. [AJ#2978]

MOWATT, HAROLD JOHN, Lieutenant of the 64th Regiment, died in St Croix 1801. [AJ#2807]

MUNN, DONALD, Corporal of the Black Watch, land grant by the Nashwaak River, New Brunswick, 1785. [PANB: MC315]

MUNRO, GEORGE, Lieutenant Colonel of Otway's Regiment of Foot, Commander in Chief at Fort William Henry on Lake George, died in Albany, New York, 9.1758. [SM.19.669]

MUNRO, WILLIAM, soldier of the Black Watch, land grant by the Nashwaak River, New Brunswick, 1785. [PANB:MC315]

MURCHISON, JOHN R. M., third son of Kenneth Murchison in Inverness, Captain of the 3rd Regiment of Foot, died 6.1.1850. [Spanish Town Cathedral, Jamaica, g/s]

MURRAY, JAMES, a former Captain of the Queen's American Rangers, died in Norfolk, Virginia, 29.3.1789. [Scots Magazine #51.361]

MURRAY, JOHN, Major, land grant in West Florida 19.10.1770.
[Acts.PCCol.V.594]

NAIRNE, Captain THOMAS, a reduced officer, applied for a land grant
of 20,000 acres in Quebec 9.11.1764. [JCTP.1765.185; 1766.151]

NAUGHTY, JOHN, born in Scotland 1732, a planter in Stafford County,
Virginia, a militiaman of the Virginia Regiment 1757.
[VMHB.1/2][L]

PATULLO, THOMAS, Paymaster of the 93rd Regiment of Foot, died in
Antigua 18.4.1827. [AJ#4143]

PAUL, HUGH, born in Scotland 1731, a militiaman of the Virginia
Regiment 1757. [VMHB.1/2][L]

PEEBLES, GEORGE, soldier of the Black Watch, and wife, land grant by
the Nashwaak River, New Brunswick, 1785. [PANB: MC315]

PEEBLES, JOHN, soldier of the Black Watch, land grant by the
Nashwaak River, New Brunswick, 1785. [PANB: MC315]

PERRY, CHARLES, Colonel of the 55th Regiment of Foot, raised in
Scotland 1756, died in Halifax, Nova Scotia, 7.1757. [SM.19.438]

POLSON, WILLIAM, son of John Polson and Janet Mackay in Navidale,
Sutherland, Captain of the Virginia Rangers, died at the
Monogahela River, Virginia, 1755. [Book of Mackay, 295]

PONTON, Lieutenant THOMAS, son of Alexander Ponton an architect in
Edinburgh, died at Fort Haldane, Jamaica, 1801. [AJ#2822]

RAMSAY, ALEXANDER, born 1791, third son of Captain Ramsay of
the Royal Navy, died in New Orleans 1.1.1815. [Musselburgh g/s]

REID, JOHN, born 13.2.1721 son of Baron Reid of Straloch, an officer of
Loudoun's Highlanders 1745-, served under Wolfe and Amherst,
fought in Martinique, member of the St Andrew's Society of New
York 1762, married Susannah Alexander in New York 28.12.1762,
to Fort Pitt 1763, fought at Bushy Run, General of the 88th
Regiment 1798, died in London 6.2.1807. [ANY.1.30]

ROBERTSON, DONALD, soldier of the Black Watch, land grant by the
Nashwaak River, New Brunswick, 1785. [PANB: MC315]

ROBERTSON, JAMES, Newbigging, Fife, Lieutenant General, probate
22.3.1788 New York

ROBERTSON, JOHN, Lieutenant of the 42nd Regiment at Albany,
Montreal and New York, 1759-1762. [SRO.GD132]

ROBERTSON, JOHN, soldier of the Black Watch, land grant by the
Nashwaak River, New Brunswick, 1785. [PANB: MC315]

ROBERTSON of STRUAN, Colonel, late of the 82nd Regiment,
allocated 1600 acres in Nova Scotia 1784. [HP115]

ROBINSON, JAMES, born in Scotland 1735, a shoemaker in King
George County, Virginia, a militiaman of the Virginia Regiment
1757. [VMHB.1/2][L]

ROBINSON, JOHN, born in Scotland 1736, a planter in Fredericksburg,
Virginia, a militiaman of the Virginia Regiment 1757.
[VMHB.1/2][L]

ROBSON, JOHN, Corporal of the 82nd Foot, shipped to America 1778,
stationed at Halifax, Nova Scotia, fought in the American War of
Independence, demobilised in 1783, given a land grant in Pictou
County, Nova Scotia. [SG.33.2.203]

ROSE, DONALD, soldier of the Black Watch, land grant by the
Nashwaak River, New Brunswick, 1785. [PANB: MC315]

ROSE, JOHN, born 1803, Ensign of the 70th Foot, son of Major Rose of
the 6th Royal Veteran Battalion, died in Amherstburg, Upper
Canada, 21.1.1827. [AJ#4135]

ROSS, ANDREW, soldier of the Black Watch, land grant by the
Nashwaak River, New Brunswick, 1785. [PANB: MC315]

ROSS, DONALD, soldier of the Black Watch, wife and 2 children, land
grant by the Nashwaak River, New Brunswick, 1785. [PANB:
MC315]

ROSS, D.M., former Captain of the 34th Regiment of Foot, resident in
Lasswade, applied to settle in Canada 26.5.1819. [PRO.CO.384]

ROSS, JAMES, sr., soldier of the Black Watch, wife and 1 child, land
grant by the Nashwaak River, New Brunswick, 1785. [PANB:
MC315]

ROSS, JAMES, jr., soldier of the Black Watch, land grant by the
Nashwaak River, New Brunswick, 1785. [PANB:MC315]

ROSS, JOHN, Lieutenant of the 71st Regiment of Grenadiers, a prisoners
of the Americans, in New York 3.1781. [SRO.RH15.44.103]

ROSS, WILLIAM, born in Scotland 1731, a planter in Caroline County,
Virginia, a militiaman of the Virginia Regiment 1757.
[VMHB.1/2][L]

SALMON, GEORGE, born in Scotland 1727, a planter in Stafford
County, Virginia, a militiaman of the Virginia Regiment 1757.
[VMHB.1/2][L]

SCOTT, JAMES, born in Scotland 1704, a smith in Norfolk, Virginia, a
militiaman of the Virginia Regiment 1756. [VMHB.1/2][L]

SCOTT, JOHN, born in Scotland 1718, a planter in Prince William
County, Virginia, a militiaman of the Virginia Regiment 1757.
[VMHB.1/2][L]

SCOTT, JOHN, born in Scotland 1728, a sailor in Prince William County, Virginia, a militiaman of the Virginia Regiment 1757. [VMHB.1/2][L]

SCOTT, THOMAS, paymaster of the 70th Regiment, son of Walter Scott W.S., died in Quebec 14.2.1823. [EEC#117433]

SHAW, Lieutenant ALEXANDER, Adjutant of the 60th Royal American Regiment of Foot, 6.10.1761. [SRO.GD103.2.412]

SHERIFF, CHARLES, Lieutenant of the 45th Regiment, given a land grant in New York 1773. [PCCol.V.597]

SIMPSON, C.A., assistant surgeon of the 60th Light Infantry, died in Annapolis Royal, Nova Scotia, 20.3.1820. [S.4.177]

SINCLAIR, CHARLES, former Ensign of the 78th (Fraser Highlanders) Regiment, received a land grant in New York 1773. [PC.Col.5.597]

SMALL, JOHN, born in Strathardle, Perthshire, 1726, officer of the Scotch Brigade in Dutch Service, officer of the 42nd Regiment 1756-1763, at Ticonderoga 1758, on the expedition to Lake Champlain and from Oswego to Montreal, in the West Indies 1762, member of the St Andrew's Society of New York 1763, returned to America as an officer of the 21st (Royal North British Fusiliers) Regiment, Major of the 84th (Royal Highland Emigrants) 1775, at Bunker Hill, at Battle of Eutaw Springs, quartered on Long Island 1782, Major General 1794, died in Guernsey 17.3.1796. [ANY.1.55]

SMITH, LAUCHLAN, born in Inverness, served under Wolfe at the capture of Quebec 1762, died in Quebec 29.6.1823. [Scotsman#380.360]

SPITTAL, JOHN, at Fort Lawrence, Chigneto, Nova Scotia, 1750. [SRO.GD172.1630]

STEWART, ALEXANDER, born in Scotland 1736, a planter in Stafford County, Virginia, a militiaman of the Virginia Regiment 1756. [VMHB.1/2][L]

STEWART, DUNCAN, soldier of the Black Watch, land grant by the Nashwaak River, New Brunswick, 1785. [PANB: MC315]

STEWART, JAMES, of Urrard, Perthshire, Captain of the 2nd Battalion of the 42nd {Royal Highlanders} Regiment, wounded at Ticonderoga 1758. [ANY.1.29]

STEWART, JOHN, emigrated from Greenock to Boston on the Glasgow Packet, Captain Arthur Porterfield, in September 1775, enlisted into the 84th (Royal Highland Emigrants) Regiment 23 October 1775. [SRO.GD174.2093]

STEWART, KENNETH, Edinburgh, Captain in the late North Carolina Highlanders, pro.7.1815 PCC

STEWART, PETER, Sergeant of the Black Watch, wife and 3 children, land grant on the Nashwaak River, New Brunswick, 1785. [PANB: MC315]

STEWART, PETER, of the Prince Edward Island Fencibles and of the Royal Artillery, 1799-1837. [SRO.NRAS.2178.1]

STEWART, ROBERT, born in Scotland 1736, a planter in Stafford County, Virginia, a militiaman of the Virginia Regiment 1757. [VMHB.1/2][L]

SPROWLE, ANDREW, Sergeant of the Black Watch, wife and 2 children, land grant by the Nashwaak River, New Brunswick, 1785. [PANB: MC315]

STEWART, JOHN, soldier of the Black Watch, land grant by the Nashwaak River, New Brunswick, 1785. [PANB: MC315]

STOBO, ..., Glasgow, former Captain of the 15th Regiment, settled at Seignory Aux Loutres, Lake Champlain and Otter Creek, before 1775. [PC.Col.5.147]

SUTHERLAND, GEORGE, soldier of the Black Watch, land grant by the Nashwaak River, New Brunswick, 1785. [PANB: MC315]

SUTHERLAND, HUGH, soldier of the Black Watch, land grant by the Nashwaak River, New Brunswick, 1785. [PANB:MC315]

SUTHERLAND, JOHN, {1}, soldier of the Black Watch, land grant by the Nashwaak River, New Brunswick, 1785. [PANB:MC315]

SUTHERLAND, JOHN, {2}, soldier of the Black Watch, land grant by the Nashwaak River, New Brunswick, 1785. [PANB: MC315]

SUTHERLAND, PATRICK, younger son of James Sutherland of Clyne and Jean Gordon, Officer of Oglethorpe's Regiment in Georgia 1738-1745, British Army officer in Nova Scotia - possibly died there 1766. [SG.XLI.2][PRO.CO5.668.130/1; 282/3]

SUTHERLAND, JOHN, {3}, soldier of the Black Watch, land grant by the Nashwaak River, New Brunswick, 1785. [PANB: MC315]

SUTHERLAND, ROBERT, soldier of the Black Watch, wife and 2 children, land grant by the Nashwaak River, New Brunswick, 1785. [PANB: MC315]

SUTHERLAND, WILLIAM, Sergeant in the 77th Regiment of Foot 1756-1764, discharged in New York, received a land grant near Fort Ticonderoga, Crown Point, New York, Loyalist. [PRO.AO13.15.487/491]

SUTHERLAND, WILLIAM, soldier of the Black Watch, wife and 3 children, land grant by the Nashwaak River, New Brunswick, 1785. [PANB: MC315]

THOMAS, JAMES, born in Scotland 1725, a sailmaker in Alexandria, Virginia, a militiaman of the Virginia Regiment 1757. [VMHB.1/2][L]

THOMS, JAMES, born in Scotland 1730, a farmer and a militiaman of the Virginia Regiment 1753. [VMHB.1/2]

THOMSON, JOHN, Sergeant of the Black Watch, land grant by the Nashwaak River, New Brunswick, 1785. [PANB:MC315]

THOMPSON, JOHN, private of the 1st Battalion of the 1st Royal Regiment, in St Domingo 1796, at capture of Port au Prince, died 1797. [SRO.GD21.643.1/4]

THOMPSON, THOMAS, born in Scotland 1724, a schoolmaster in Winchester County, Virginia, a militiaman of the Virginia Regiment 1756. [VMHB.1/2]

TRAVIS, CHARLES, born in Scotland 1733, a planter in Richmond, Virginia, a militiaman of the Virginia Regiment 1756. [VMHB.1/2][L]

TROTTER, RICHARD, born in Scotland 1726, a mason in Essex County, Virginia, a militiaman of the Virginia Regiment 1756. [VMHB.1/2][L]

TURNBULL, GEORGE, born in Perthshire, Ensign in General Marjorybank's Scots Regiment - discharged 18.4.1756, an officer in the 60th [Royal American] Regiment 1756-1772, and in the New York Volunteers, settled in New York 1788, died 13.10.1810 in Bloomingdale, New York. [ANY.1.48][SRO.B59.38.6.263]

UMLACH, JOHN, born in Elgin 2.8.1726, emigrated to Philadelphia before 1757, soldier of the 60th[Royal American] Regiment 1757-1763, settled in Chester, Nova Scotia, 11.1764, died 6.7.1821. [NSHR.X.35]

URQUHART, GEORGE RODERICK, Lieutenant of the 33rd Regiment of Foot, son of Reverend John Urquhart of Mounteagle, minister of Fearn, Ross-shire, died in Falmouth, Jamaica, 27.3.1825. [AJ#4041]

WALTERS, ROBERT, born in Scotland 1734, a planter in Northumberland County, Virginia, a militiaman of the Virginia Regiment 1756. [VMHB.1/2][L]

WARDROBE, ALEXANDER, Lieutenant of the 43rd Regiment, son of David Wardrobe a surgeon in Edinburgh, died in St Pierre, Martinique, 10.8.1799. [AJ#2700]

WARDROPE, WILLIAM, former Lieutenant Colonel of the 47th Regiment, died on St Simon's Island, Georgia, 1812. [Edinburgh Advertiser#5129.13]

WEBSTER, ALEXANDER, Captain of the 5oth Regiment of Foot, died in Montreal 25.5.1820. [Scotsman.4.178]

WEBSTER, DAVID, Musselburgh, a gunner's mate, died in Virginia, pro. 2.1767 PCC

WEIR, JOHN, Royal Commissary General for the Forces in Dominica, cnf 24.1.1781 Commissariot of Edinburgh

WEIR, JOHN, soldier of the Black Watch, and wife, land grant by the Nashwaak River, New Brunswick, 1785. [PANB: MC315]

WHITE, WILLIAM, born in Scotland 1708, a planter at Fort Cumberland, Maryland, a militiaman of the Virginia Regiment 1758. [VMHB.1/2][L]

WHITELAW, THOMAS, born 1.10.1791, surgeon in the Royal Artillery, died in Barbados 22.10.1849. [Musselburgh g/s]

WILSON, ADAM, soldier of the Black Watch, land grant on the Nashwaak River, New Brunswick, 1785. [PANB: MC315]

WISHART, ALEXANDER, Lieutenant on half pay, 42nd Regiment, died in Upper Canada 10.12.1823. [Fife Herald#113]

YELDEN, ALEXANDER, Sergeant of the Black Watch, wife and child, land grant by the Nashwaak River, New Brunswick, 1785. [PANB:MC315]

YOUNG, JAMES, born in Scotland 1718, a merchant in Albemarle County, Virginia, a militiaman of the Virginia Regiment 1756. [VMHB.1/2][L]

YOUNG, WILLIAM, born in Edinburgh, a surgeon in the British Army, married Elizabeth Clauson in Annapolis Royal, Nova Scotia, 5.1.1785, settled on Staten Island, New York. [ANY.II.43]

# REFERENCES

## ARCHIVES

| | | | |
|---|---|---|---|
| PANB | Public Archives of New Brunswick | | |
| PRO | Public Record Office | | |
| | | AO | Audit Office |
| | | CO | Colonial Office |
| | | PCC | Prerogative Court of Canterbury |
| SRO | Scottish Record Office | | |
| | | B | Burgh Records |
| | | CC | Commissariat Court |
| | | GD | Gifts & Deposits |
| | | NRAS | Natl. Reg. Archives, Scotland |

## PUBLICATIONS

| | |
|---|---|
| AJ | Aberdeen Journal |
| ANY | Biographical Register of St Andrews Society of New York |
| ANQ | Aberdeen Notes & Queries |
| BM | Book of Mackay |
| CD | Clan Donald |
| EEC | Edinburgh Evening Courant |
| F | Fastii Ecclesiae Scoticanae |
| HA | History of the town of Antigonish |
| HP | History of the County of Pictou, Nova Scotia |
| JAHR | Journal of Army Historical Research |
| JCTP | Journal of the Committee on Trade and the Plantations |
| L | Virginia Colonial Soldiers |
| NSHR | Nova Scotia Historical Review |
| PCCol | Acts of the Privy Council, Colonial |
| S | The Scotsman |
| SG | Scottish Genealogist |
| SM | Scots Magazine |
| VaGaz | Virginia Gazette |
| VMHB | Virginia Magazine of History & Biography |
| WMQ | William & Mary Quarterly |

"Deserted from the 2nd Battalion of Royals at Fort George, James Robinson aged 16, 5 foot, 4 inches, born in America, a labourer, with fair hair, grey eyes, fresh complexion, wearing a brown camblet coat, a grey waistcoat, leather breeches and a small round hat. One guinea reward" Aberdeen Journal#1567, January 1778

Lightning Source UK Ltd.
Milton Keynes UK
UKHW022050060720
366115UK00017B/268